MW01273862

Six Chapters of a Floating Life

浮生六记

外语教学与研究出版社
FOREIGN LANGUAGE TEACHING AND RESEARCH PRESS
北京 BEIJING

[清] 沈复 著　林语堂 译
ENGLISH WORKS OF LIN YUTANG
林语堂英文作品集

京权图字：01-98-0342

ⓒ 林语堂

本书由林相如女士授权外语教学与研究出版社在中国大陆独家出版、发行。
版权所有，翻版必究。

图书在版编目(CIP)数据

　　浮生六记 = Six Chapters of a Floating Life: 汉英对照／(清)沈复著；林语堂
译 . — 北京：外语教学与研究出版社，2009.6
　　(林语堂英文作品集)
　　ISBN 978-7-5600-8705-4

　　Ⅰ . 浮… 　Ⅱ . ①沈… ②林… 　Ⅲ . 古典散文—作品集—中国—清代—英文
Ⅳ . I264.9

中国版本图书馆 CIP 数据核字 (2009) 第 094584 号

出　版　人：于春迟
照片提供：台北"林语堂故居"
　　　　　福建漳州"林语堂纪念馆"
责任编辑：周　晶
装帧设计：视觉共振
出版发行：外语教学与研究出版社
社　　址：北京市西三环北路 19 号 (100089)
网　　址：http://www.fltrp.com
印　　刷：紫恒印装有限公司
开　　本：880×1230　1/32
印　　张：11.375　彩插：0.5
版　　次：2009 年 7 月第 1 版　2009 年 7 月第 1 次印刷
书　　号：ISBN 978-7-5600-8705-4
定　　价：22.90 元
＊　　＊　　＊
如有印刷、装订质量问题出版社负责调换
制售盗版必究　举报查实奖励
版权保护办公室举报电话：(010)88817519
物料号：187050001

出 版 说 明

"两脚踏东西文化，一心评宇宙文章；挚爱故国不泥古，乐享生活不流俗。"——林语堂的作品如同他的一生，孜孜地向世界解说中国，向祖国表达赤忱。选择林语堂的作品重印出版，首先是因为他向西方介绍中国文化的贡献。作为用外语创作的一位中国作家，他的系列作品影响深远，被视作阐述东方思想的重要著述。其次，还因为他非凡的文学造诣，作为国际笔会的副会长，并获诺贝尔文学奖的提名，林语堂赢得了世界文坛的尊重，也为中国人赢得了骄傲。再者，应是惊叹于他那"极其美妙，令以英文为母语的人既羡慕敬佩又深感惭愧"的英语了；而且，今天我们终于让林先生不再遗憾"……三十年著作全用英文，应是文字精华所在，惜未能与中国读者相见……"

这次结集的"林语堂英文作品集"，除保留我社曾出版的《吾国与吾民》、《生活的艺术》和《京华烟云》等代表作品外，还收录了《风声鹤唳》、《老子的智慧》和《武则天传》等十余部颇具影响的原版著作。如此规模的林语堂英文作品在国内出版尚属首次，包括其中几种是首次以英文原貌在国内面世。此外，为了更好地介绍和呈现林语堂及其作品，我们还从台北林语堂故居和漳州林语堂纪念馆等地采集珍贵图片（林语堂故居 60 余幅，林语堂纪念馆 10 余幅），如林语堂生平不同时期的独照、与亲友的合影、部分手稿和初版封面的存照等，以飨读者。

　　林语堂用美妙的英文向世界介绍中国人和中国历史文化，但是，囿于所处时代、社会环境和个人经历，他的思想认识不免带有历史的局限。20 世纪 30 年代至 50 年代正是中国国内动荡变迁、破旧立新的时期，特定的创作背景无疑也给他的作品留下印痕。显而易见地，比如当时对朝代称谓与历史纪元的划定不统一（如称清朝为 Manchu Dynasty）；且时无汉语拼音方案，专有名词均使用威妥玛拼音音译等。此外，也能发现作者在解读文化历史和社会生活现象时的不足，如反映在民族关系的表述上，称中国的一些少数民族为 foreign blood、foreign race，乃至以 Chinese 特指 Han Chinese 等。诸如此类，为不妨碍我们对文学和语言的鉴赏，在我们最大程度地保留作品原貌的同时，敬期读者明辨。

Lin Yutang just arrived at Shanghai for his further education.

Lin Yutang and his family went to the United States by sea, and stopped at Los Angels on their way.

Lin Yutang in Shanghai in the 1930s

Lin Yutang, about 1936 (Original size: 18.5cm×24.5cm)

Mr. Lin in New York, about 1937
(Photographer: Carl Van Vechten; Original size: 20.3cm×25.4cm)

The Lin couple in New York, 1937
(Photographer: Carl Van Vechten; Original size: 19.7cm×24.2cm)

Lin Yutang stood in front of Xu Beihong's painting *The Horse* in New York, about 1940. (Photographer: Pix Incorporated; Original size: 19.3cm×24.3cm)

王欽於川相館

Air Port Studio
Manila

The Lin family stopped by Manila on their way back to China in 1940.

Lin Yutang demonstrated how to use the "Chinese Fast Typewriter" in New York, 1948.
(Original size: 13cm×9cm)

Lin Yutang at home in New York, about 1948
(Photographer: Elli Marcus; Original size: 20.7cm×25.4cm)

The Lin couple in the 1940s

The Lin couple receiving a warm welcome in Singapore in the 1950s

Lin Yutang in the United States in the 1950s

The Lin couple, 1955 (Original size: 6cm×9cm)

The Lin couple, 1965 (Original size: 7.7cm×5.1cm)

The Lin couple with friend, 1968 (Original size: 17.9cm×12.9cm)

During June 18-20, 1968, the Lin couple were invited to the Conference of the International Association of University Presidents in Seoul.

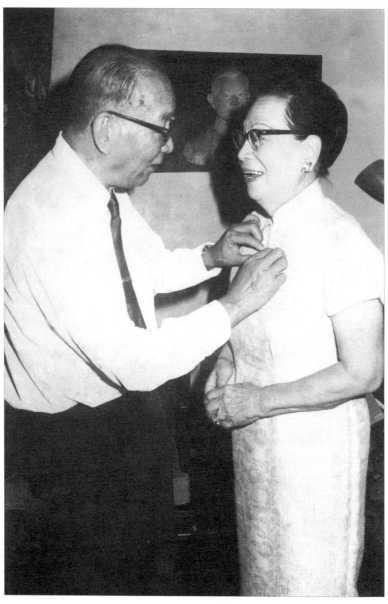

Lin Yutang pinning a gold brooch for his wife Liao Cuifeng as a 50th-anniversary wedding gift at their Yangmingshan residence, 1969.
(Original size: 10cm×14.2cm)

Lin Yutang delivered a speech at Sogang University, Seoul, 1970. (Original size: 14.1cm×11.4cm)

SIX CHAPTERS OF
A FLOATING LIFE

浮生六记

CONTENTS

FOREWORD

One morning in 1905, or the 31th year of the reign of Emperor Guangxu of Qing Dynasty, two brothers set out by boat from their hometown Boa-ah, a mountain hamlet in Fujian province on the southern coast of China, for the port city of Xiamen, some sixty miles away. The boys were full of excitement and chatter, especially the younger one. Yutang was ten years old, and today, he was taking leave of his hometown and going with his brother to study in Xiamen. They were sons of Pastor Lin Zhicheng, who was born in the poor village of Wulisha. Pastor Lin was sending his sons to free missionary schools in Xiamen.

The Pastor was not a follower of convention, so the boys did not wear queues. Yutang was a little guy, deeply tanned, with a prominent forehead, a pair of sparkling eyes, and a narrow chin. Six miles later, when the skiff came to Xiaoxi, the boys changed to a five-sail junk, and sailed toward Zhangzhou on West River. There were paddy fields and farmhouses on either side of the river, and tall mountains stood behind them, clad in grey-purplish hues. Yutang thought it inexpressibly beautiful. After a day's journey, the junk tied up against the bank under some bamboo trees. Yutang was told to lie down, cover himself with a blanket and go to sleep.

But sleep was the last thing on the boy's mind. The boatman sitting at the junk's stern was sucking at his pipe, and between gulps of bitter tea, telling stories about the Empress Dowager Cexi, who ruled the court today, having put the Emperor Guangxu under house arrest for supporting the reformers at the palace. Another junk was tied up on the opposite bank, brightly lit by lanterns. A soft breeze wafted sounds of merrymaking and music from a lute across the water. Oh, what a beautiful scene! Yutang thought, I must remember this evening well, so that the sights and sounds will always be fresh in my mind when I recall this night, however old I might be.

At the thought of going to school in Xiamen, his heart leapt with anticipation. He often went to watch the sunset behind the tall mountains which completely surrounded the hamlet. The mountain peaks were always shrouded in clouds. How did a person get out of this deep valley, he wondered. What was the world like outside? To the north there was a crack in one of the peaks, left there, it was said, when a fairy stubbed his toe on a rock. The world was so big that it boggled his mind. Two years ago, his father told him the first airplane had a successful test flight. "I've read everything I could lay my hands on about the airplane," his father said, "but I've never seen one, and I don't know whether I should believe it." His father also told him that the best universities in the world were the University of Berlin in Germany, and Oxford University in England. "You must study hard, young man," his father often said, sitting beside the boy's bed at night, turning up the oil lamp and smoking his pipe. "Study hard, so that you can go to one of those universities. Acquire an education and become a famous man."

My father often repeated this story to me. As I sat in his study, surrounded by bookshelves of his works, I knew that Grandfather's words were the inspiration of his life. In his 80 years, my father wrote and translated more than 50 books and became a world-renowned author. The *New York Times* said at the time of his death, "Lin Yutang had no peer as an interpreter to Western minds of the customs, aspirations, fears and thought of his people." Father was a novelist, essayist, philosopher, philologist and lexicographer. He also invented a Chinese typewriter. "But he was more," wrote Prof. Nelson I. Wu of Washington University in St. Louis, Missouri. "He was a total man, stubbornly going his own way through the criticism of lesser minds to become a universal genius."

Father was born in 1895, the fifth of six sons of Lin Zhicheng. The Presbyterian pastor, a self-taught man, communicated to his children a passionate zest for all that was new and modern from the West, and decided that his sons must learn English and receive Western educations. With the help of one of his brothers and a loan, Yutang attended St. John's University in Shanghai. The main emphasis was on English. Yutang also studied theology, because he wanted to be a pastor like his father. But after extensive reading in science, he began to have doubts about Christian dogma, and changed his major to philosophy.

When he graduated from St. John's in 1916, Yutang accepted a teaching post at Qinghua College in Beijing. Here, he found himself surrounded by Chinese history, and he realized how small the confines of his Christian education had been. He knew that Joshua's trumpet blew down the walls of Jericho, but did not know the folktale of Meng Jiangnü, whose tears for her lost husband at the Great Wall caused a section of the wall to collapse and expose his dead body. Determined to make up for his inadequacy, Yutang haunted bookstores, asking shopkeepers what were the most important books to read, because he was too ashamed to ask others.

When he was not reading, Yutang tried to devise a better method for looking up characters in a Chinese dictionary than the prevailing Kangxi method, the bane of scholars and students alike. At the age of 23, he published *An Index System for Chinese Characters* for which Cai Yuanpei, chancellor of National University of Peking (Beida), wrote a preface. The work attracted the attention of scholars and was a catalyst for change. But Yutang was already dissatisfied with his method, and he continued throughout his life to work on improvements. These were finally incorporated in his monumental Chinese-English dictionary published when he was 77 years old.

Yutang taught at Qinghua for three years, then qualified to study in America. He received a half-scholarship to major in modern languages at Harvard Graduate School of Arts & Sciences. In 1919, he married Liao Cuifeng from Xiamen, and took his bride with him to Cambridge, Massachusetts. At the end of the year, his stipend stopped coming, and he had not enough money to get his Master's degree at Harvard.

World War I was now over. China had sent some 150,000 laborers to France, and Yutang accepted a job at the American YMCA [Young Men's Christian Association] to teach the laborers to read and write. The couple moved to Le Creusot, a small town in France. When they had saved some money, Yutang had taught himself German, and they went to the University of Jena in Germany because the living standard there was lower. Yutang took courses and transferred credit to receive his Master's from Harvard. To the dean of Harvard Graduate School he wrote in 1920, "I do not wish to plead for any special leniency in giving me the degree. Nor am I going to be intellectually arrested myself after I should get the degree. It is for the reason of great practical utility that I wish to have this certificate. I believe that the Harvard degree will make my progress through the German University much quicker and easier." In 1923, he received his Ph.D. in Philology from Leipzig University, and returned to China.

The country was in turmoil. Politically, China was in the grip of feudal warlords who fought one another incessantly. Yutang, a professor in the English Department of Beida, wrote articles and criticized the corrupt and ineffective government. The feuding warlords fought on. Duan Qirui ordered the arrest of some 50 professors and newspapermen who criticized the government. Yutang's name was on the list. Two editors who were arrested were shot in the same night.

By now my parents had two daughters, my older sister and myself. We left for Xiamen, where Father joined the faculty of Xiamen University as dean of the College of Arts and Letters. But, university politics made it impossible for him to stay on, and a year later, he joined the Ministry of Foreign Affairs in the Wuhan Government, because he admired Foreign Minister Chen Yuren, whom he had known in Beijing. When the Wuhan Government was toppled in 1927, Father quit his job, and we moved to Shanghai.

Here, he began to write the enormously successful *Kaiming English Books*, a series that was adopted as textbooks for middle schools. With his founding of the *Analects* bi-monthly in 1932 in Shanghai, Father made his reputation in China. The magazine specialized in humor and satire, but it was Father's contributions that most captured the readers. Poking fun at government officials, he once said, "Although you are an official, you still *look* like a man."

Father's lacerating wit earned him the reputation of *enfant terrible* and the accolade "Master of Humor." In 1934 and 1935, he started two more magazines, *This Human World* and *The Cosmic Wind*. Also at this time, Father was writing an English column called "The Little Critic" which appeared in *China Critic* magazine, as well as editing a Chinese dictionary in the style of the *Concise Oxford Dictionary*. At the same time, he was translating English works into Chinese, such as the biography of Henrik Ibsen and George Bernard Shaw's *Pygmalion*. And he was translating Chinese into English, the most notable work of which was Qing Dynasty author Shen Fu's *Six Chapters of a Floating Life*, which was published in bilingual form in Shanghai in 1935. The author wrote about the idyllic life he led with his wife Yun, whom Father described in a preface as "one of the loveliest of women in Chinese literature." The story and the translation received wide attention.

Father's "Little Critic" essays caught the attention of Pearl S. Buck, who was living in China, and whose novel *The Good Earth* had won the Pulitzer Prize. One evening the two writers met. They had been speaking of foreign writers in China, when Father suddenly said, "I should like to write a book telling exactly what I feel about China."

"You are the one to do it," Mrs. Buck replied enthusiastically.

Father finished the book in 1935, and it was called *My Country and My People*. In the book, Father surveyed the mental and moral constitution and ideals of the Chinese people, as well as society, literature and the art of living. "China is too big a country, and her national life has too many facets for her not to be open to the most diverse interpretations," he wrote. "I can lay bare her troubles because I have not lost hope."

The politically motivated writers lost no time in tearing the book apart, but Father was not bothered. "If a man must be a writer," he said, "he should have some courage and speak his mind." He had nothing but contempt for literary prostitutes who owed their living to political bosses.

"The book burst like a shell over the Western world," according to the *New York Times*. "*My Country and My People* is the clearest and most interesting dissection and synthesis of China past and present that I have read," wrote Fanny Butcher in the *Chicago Daily Tribune*. "One of the most important and satisfactory books yet written in English on the character, life and philosophy of the Chinese people," wrote W. L. Langer in *Foreign Affairs*. "No one who wants to know either old or new China need go beyond the covers of *My Country and My People*... The whole gamut of matters Chinese is here treated with a deftness, a frankness, an intelligence, a subtlety seldom matched in any work," wrote T. F. Opie in *Churchman*.

Father was 41. Success did not change him. "I am still a child, looking at this extraordinary world with round eyes," he said. "There is so much I must learn; everything arouses my curiosity. I have only one interest, and that is to know more about life, past and present, and to write about it. I would not like fame if it gets in the way."

In 1936, our family, which now included three daughters, went to America, intending to stay only a year. But when the Sino-Japanese War broke out the next year, we had to delay our return. Father was horrified to learn the 52 manuscript volumes of the Chinese dictionary he was editing, which he had not brought to the States, had been destroyed.

In New York, Father began to write *The Importance of Living*, one of his most famous books and a grand synthesis of his philosophy. It became the best-selling book in America in 1938, was translated into a dozen languages, and secured for him the position of a leading interpreter of China to the West. In comparing East and West, he found no difference so sharp as the attitude toward old age. "I am still continually shocked by the Western attitude," he wrote. "I heard an old lady remark that she had several grandchildren, 'but it was the first one that *hurt*.' Even with the knowledge that Americans hate to be thought of as old, one still doesn't quite expect to have it put that way."

On the importance of the home, he wrote, "It has seemed to me that the final test of any civilization is, what type of husbands and wives and fathers and mothers does it turn out. Besides the austere simplicity of such a question, every other achievement of civilization—art, philosophy, literature and material living—pales into insignificance."

"Dr. Lin has performed the inestimable service of distilling the philosophy of generations of Chinese sages and presenting it against a modern… background, which makes it easily readable and understandable," said *The Saturday Review of Literature*.

Moment in Peking, published in 1940, was a novel of broad canvas which began with the Boxer Rebellion in 1901 and ended with the beginning of the Sino-Japanese War. Like *The Importance of Living*, it became a selection of the Book-of-the-Month Club. It "may well become the classic background novel of modern China", said *Time* magazine.

Father's books were translated into Chinese and well-received, although he was not always pleased with the translations. "My regret is that I did not, through most of my works, meet my readers face to face," he said toward the end of his life, referring to the fact that most of his works' Chinese translations were done by others.

But he was too busy creatively to translate. After the war ended, Father embarked upon an adventure that was to wipe out all his assets and get him deeply in debt. He decided to build a Chinese typewriter that anyone could use without previous training. Because he had written and edited a string of well-received books, including *The Wisdom of China and India* in 1942, he felt he could afford this project. In fact, he had been trying to invent a typewriter ever since he went to Peking in the 1920s. Never mind that Chinese consisted of tens of thousands of ideographs while English had only 26 letters of the alphabet, he thought it could be done.

His solution lay in finding a better way to classify Chinese characters than the Kangxi system. He thought he had the problem solved back in 1931, when he tried to have a model of his invention made in London. But he had run out of funds and returned home with only 30 cents in his pocket.

Now, working like a man possessed, Father was up at dawn and did not go to bed until after midnight. He drew sketches, rearranged characters and redesigned his keyboard. In New York's Chinatown, he found a printer who could mold the characters. Then, he located a small engineering firm to help him with the mechanics and a workshop to produce the parts. Problem after problem had to be overcome, and the bills mounted. Each of the thousand parts was made by hand. But he had sunk so much money into the machine that he could not give up. As their savings vanished, Mother was horrified. But she knew her husband well. He was easygoing about many things, but obstinated about some things, and inventing a typewriter was one of them.

Fortunately, Father had a friend in antique dealer Loo Chin-tsai, who loaned him tens of thousands of dollars to finish the model. Finally, in May 1947, we brought his invention home. It was called the Mingkwai ("clear and quick") Typewriter. The machine had 72 keys. To type a character, one pressed the keys corresponding to the top and bottom parts of a character, and those with similar tops and bottoms appeared on a screen in the center of the machine. The typist then pressed one of eight printing keys according to the position of the correct character on the screen. At a time when computers had not yet become popular, his invention of a scanning screen was remarkable. The typefaces were molded around six hexagonal rollers. No larger than a standard typewriter, the Mingkwai typed 7,000 whole characters and by combinations a theoretical total of 90,000.

The typewriter was presented at a press conference held at home, and received great write-ups in the press. Dr. George A. Kennedy, director,

Institute of Far East Languages, Yale University, said that "the finding system is the most efficient yet devised, and it may well be extended to dictionaries and other reference works."

Lee Tuh-Yueh, manager of the Bank of China in New York, said, "I was not prepared for anything so compact and at the same time comprehensive, so easy to operate and yet so adequate." And Father's good friend, the philologist Yuen R. Chao, simply said, "Y. T., I think this is it!"

But Father was deeply in debt. One day I came home from Columbia University where I was attending classes, and found Mother in tears. Although we were in touch with many typewriter companies, we could not hope for quick results. China was in the midst of civil war, and the largest potential market was uncertain.

Sometime later, when we were riding in a taxi and Father was playing with a cardboard mockup of the keyboard, he said, "The crux of the invention is here. The mechanical problems were not hard."

"Then, could you have just used this mockup to sell your invention? Was there any need to build the model?" I asked.

He looked at me for a few seconds. "I suppose I could have," he whispered, "but I couldn't help myself. I had to make a real typewriter. I never dreamed it would cost so much."

The Mingkwai is never manufactured, because it was too costly to produce, and China was in turmoil. But with the coming of the computer age, the mechanical problems of a Chinese typewriter were eliminated. In 1985, the Mitac Automation Company of Taiwan bought Father's "Instant Index System," as his character classification is called, and made it the input system for its computers. "It is my legacy to the Chinese people," Father said.

Father was invited in 1948 to be the head of the Arts and Letters Division of the United Nations Educational, Scientific and Cultural Organization (UNESCO) in Paris. My parents sold their apartment in New York to pay some of their debts, and sailed for France.

At UNESCO, Father wrote memos, prepared reports and attended meetings. He found it frustrating and exhausting. "There are two kinds of animals on earth," he once wrote. "One kind minds his own business, the other minds other people's business. The former are vegetarians, like cows, sheep and thinking men. The latter are carnivorous, like hawks, tigers and men of action. I have often admired my colleagues for their administrative ability. I have never been interested in that."

He quit his job and moved to the south of France. He loved the simple life—sitting at a café and watching the fishermen's boats return with their catch, and going to market to shop for food. Life was more reasonable here than in New York. He grabbed Mother's hand and said, "Never mind, we'll start all over again. This pen of mine is still capable of earning a couple of dollars."

In 1954, Father became the first chancellor of the newly founded Nanyang University in Singapore. But, politics forced him to resign in a few months, and he and Mother returned to France. He was 60, but not feeling his age a bit. "I do not long for spring nor am I sad in the autumn," he said, "because my wife doesn't find me old."

They lived so simply that they were like children. He was writing again, and she was growing potatoes on the balcony. They took delight in the simple joys of fresh food and long walks. Later, they returned to New York to be near my sisters. In 1965, Father turned 70, and decided it was time to return to the East. A house was built for him on Yangminshan in the outskirts of Taipei, which he designed himself. He wrote a syndicated column in Chinese called "Whatever's on My Mind" (*Wu Suo Bu Tan*) which was read by five million readers around the world. In 1969, Father was made president of the Taipei Chinese Center, International P. E. N. He was nominated for the Nobel Prize for Literature in 1972 and 1973. At the time, he was working on the *Lin Yutang Chinese-English Dictionary of Modern Usage* with a small editorial staff in Taipei. The project was sponsored by the Chinese University of Hong Kong. A new Chinese-English dictionary was urgently needed to meet the demands of social and technological change.

The *Dictionary*, which Father called the crowning achievement of his career, was published in October 1972 with great fanfare. It was the first Chinese-English dictionary ever compiled by a Chinese scholar. The *New York Times* hailed it as "a milestone in communication between the world's largest linguistic groups."

On his 80th birthday, October 10, 1975, friends in Hong Kong organized a big celebration. An even bigger celebration was organized in Taipei. When I met my parents at the Hong Kong airport upon their return, Father's eyes shone with gladness. His cup was full. The only honor that he wanted and had not received was the Nobel Prize. But he was his philosophical self about it. "Let us be reasonable," he once said. "We must have an attitude of expecting neither too much nor too little from life."

Father passed away in Hong Kong on March 26 the following year. Among the many tributes he received was one by the *Reader's Digest's* founder, DeWitt Wallace. Wallace published a memorial booklet of Father's writing that had appeared over the years in the magazine. It was dedicated to the memory of "an evocative spirit of vast range and accomplishment—this man for all cultures who so enriched our lives. He considered his dictionary to be the 'crown' of his career. To anyone who reads his works, it will be apparent that Lin Yutang's crown had many jewels in it."

The *United Daily News* of Taiwan compared Father's achievements in introducing Chinese culture to the West with that of Jesuit missionary Matteo Ricci. In an editorial, the *China Times* of Taiwan said, "Dr. Lin is the scholar and writer who possibly made the greatest contribution in promoting Chinese culture internationally in the recent 100 years. For some in the West who were not well-informed, they heard about Lin Yutang before they heard about China, and heard about China before they heard about the glory of Chinese civilization."

We took his body to Taipei to be buried in the garden of his home. It has now been turned into the Lin Yutang Memorial Library, and is open to visitors. Mother passed away in 1987 at the age of 90.

I am very pleased that the Foreign Language Teaching and Research Press is now publishing in English his most distinguished works, *My Country and My People, The Importance of Living, Moment in Peking, Six Chapters of a Floating Life*, etc.

Lin Taiyi

August, 1998
Arlington, Virginia, USA

PREFACE

Yün, I think, is one of the loveliest women in Chinese literature. She is
not the most beautiful, for the author, her husband, does not make that
claim, and yet who can deny that she is the loveliest? She is just one of those
charming women one sometimes sees in the homes of one's friends, so happy
with their husbands that one cannot fall in love with them. One is glad merely
to know that such a woman exists in the world and to know her as a friend's
wife, to be accepted in her household, to be able to come uninvited to her
home for lunch, or to have her put a blanket around one's legs when one falls
asleep while she is discussing painting and literature and cucumbers in her
womanish manner with her husband. I dare say there are a number of such
women in every generation, except that in Yün I seem to feel the qualities of a
cultivated and gentle wife combined to a greater degree of perfection than falls
within our common experience. For who would not like to go out secretly with
her against her parents' wish to the Taihu Lake and see her elated at the sight
of the wide expanse of water, or watch the moon with her by the Bridge of
Ten Thousand Years? And who would not like to go with her, if she were living
in England, and visit the British Museum, where she would see the medieval
illuminated manuscripts with tears of delight? Therefore, when I say that she is
one of the loveliest women in Chinese literature and Chinese history—for she
was a real person—I do not think I have exaggerated.

Did Shen Fu, her husband, perhaps idealize her? I hardly think so. The
reader will be convinced of this when he reads the story itself. He made no
effort to whitewash her or himself. In him, too, lived the spirit of truth and
beauty and the genius for resignation and contentment so characteristic of

XIV · Six Chapters of a Floating Life

Chinese culture. I cannot help wondering what this commonplace scholar must have been like to inspire such a pure and loyal love in his wife, and to be able to appreciate it so much as to write for us one of the tenderest accounts of wedded love we have ever come across in literature. Peace be to his soul! His ancestral tomb is on the Hill of Good Fortune and Longevity in the neighbourhood of Soochow, and if we are lucky, we may still be able to find it. I do not think it would be wrong to prepare some incense and fruits and say some prayers on our knees to these two sweet souls. If I were there, I would whistle the melodies of Maurice Ravel's "Pavane," sad as death, yet smiling, or perhaps Massenet's "Melodie," tender and resigned and beautiful and purged of all exciting passions. For in the presence of these souls, one's spirit also becomes humble, not before the great, but before the small, things of life, for I truly believe that a humble life happily lived is the most beautiful thing in the universe. Inevitably, while reading and re-reading and going over this little booklet, my thoughts are led to the question of happiness. For those who do not know it, happiness is a problem, and for those who do know it, happiness is a mystery. The reading of Shen Fu's story gives one this sense of the mystery of happiness, which transcends all bodily sorrows and actual hardships—similar, I think, to the happiness of an innocent man condemned to a life-long sentence with the consciousness of having done no wrong, the same happiness that is so subtly depicted for us in Tolstoy's "Resurrection," in which the spirit conquers the body. For this reason, I think the life of this couple is one of the saddest and yet at the same time "gayest" lives, the type of gaiety that bears sorrow so well.

The Chinese title for this book is "Fousheng Liuchi" or "Six Chapters of a Floating Life," of which only four remain. (The reference is to a passage in Li Po's poem, "Our floating life is like a dream; how often can one enjoy oneself?") In form, it is unique, an autobiographical story mixed with observations and comments on the art of living, the little pleasures of life, some vivid sketches of scenery and literary and art criticism. The extant version was first published in

1877 by Yang Yinch'üan, who picked it up from a secondhand bookstore, with the two last chapters missing. According to the author's own testimony, he was born in 1763, and the fourth chapter could not have been written before 1808. A brother-in-law of Yang's and a well-known scholar, by the name of Wang T'ao, had seen the book in his childhood, so that it is likely that the book was known in the neighbourhood of Soochow in the second or third decade of the nineteenth century. From Kuan Yi-ngo's poems and from the known headings of the last chapters, we know that the Fifth Chapter recorded his experiences in Formosa [1], while the Sixth Chapter contained the author's reflections on the way of life. I have the fond hope that some complete copy of the book is still lying somewhere in some private collections or secondhand shops of Soochow, and if we are lucky, it is not altogether impossible that we may discover it still.

LIN YUTANG

Shanghai,
May 24, 1935.

---

[1] Formosa 此处指台湾。Formosa 是西方殖民者对台湾的称呼——编者注。

Chapter One

WEDDED BLISS

卷一·闺房记乐

　　余生乾隆癸未冬十一月二十有二日，正值太平盛世，且在衣冠之家，居苏州沧浪亭畔，天之厚我，可谓至矣。东坡云："事如春梦了无痕"，苟不记之笔墨，未免有辜彼苍之厚。

　　因思《关雎》冠三百篇之首，故列夫妇于首卷；余以次递及焉。所愧少年失学，稍识之无，不过记其实情实事而已。若必考订其文法，是责明于垢鉴矣。

I was born in 1763, under the reign of Ch'ienlung, on the twenty-second day of the eleventh moon. The country was then in the heyday of peace and, moreover, I was born in a scholars' family, living by the side of the Ts'anglang Pavilion in Soochow. So altogether I may say the gods have been unusually kind to me. Su Tungp'o said, "Life is like a spring dream which vanishes without a trace." I should be ungrateful to the gods if I did not try to put my life down on record.

Since the *Book of Poems* begins with a poem on wedded love, I thought I would begin this book by speaking of my marital relations and then let other matters follow. My only regret is that I was not properly educated in childhood; all I know is a simple language and I shall try only to record the real facts and real sentiments. I hope the reader will be kind enough not to scrutinize my grammar, which would be like looking for brilliance in a tarnished mirror.

余幼聘金沙于氏，八龄而夭；娶陈氏。陈名芸，字淑珍，舅氏心余先生女也。生而颖慧，学语时，口授《琵琶行》，即能成诵。四龄失怙；母金氏，弟克昌，家徒壁立。芸既长，娴女红，三口仰其十指供给；克昌从师，修脯无缺。一日，于书簏中得《琵琶行》，挨字而认，始识字；刺绣之暇，渐通吟咏，有"秋侵人影瘦，霜染菊花肥"之句。

余年十三，随母归宁，两小无嫌，得见所作，虽叹其才思隽秀，窃恐其福泽不深；然心注不能释，告母曰："若为儿择妇，非淑姊不娶。"母亦爱其柔和，即脱金约指缔姻焉；此乾隆乙未七月十六日也。

I was engaged in my childhood to one Miss Yü, of Chinsha, who died in her eighth year, and eventually I married a girl of the Ch'en clan. Her name was Yün and her literary name Suchen. She was my cousin, being the daughter of my maternal uncle, Hsinyü. Even in her childhood, she was a very clever girl, for while she was learning to speak, she was taught Po Chüyi's poem, *The P'i P'a Player*, and could at once repeat it. Her father died when she was four years old, and in the family there were only her mother (of the Chin clan) and her younger brother K'ehch'ang and herself, being then practically destitute. When Yün grew up and had learnt needlework, she was providing for the family of three, and contrived always to pay K'ehch'ang's tuition fees punctually. One day, she picked up a copy of the poem *The P'i P'a Player* from a wastebasket, and from that, with the help of her memory of the lines, she learnt to read word by word. Between her needlework, she gradually learnt to write poetry. One of her poems contained the two lines:

"*Touched by autumn, one's figure grows slender,*
Soaked in frost, the chrysanthemum blooms full."

When I was thirteen years old, I went with my mother to her maiden home and there we met. As we were two young innocent children, she allowed me to read her poems. I was quite struck by her talent, but feared that she was too clever to be happy. Still I could not help thinking of her all the time, and once I told my mother, "If you were to choose a girl for me, I won't marry any one except Cousin Su." My mother also liked her being so gentle, and gave her her gold ring as a token for the betrothal.

是年冬，值其堂姊出阁，余又随母往。

芸与余同齿而长余十月，自幼姊弟相呼，故仍呼之曰淑姊。

时但见满室鲜衣，芸独通体素淡，仅新其鞋而已。见其绣制精巧，询为己作，始知其慧心不仅在笔墨也。

其形削肩长项，瘦不露骨，眉弯目秀，顾盼神飞，唯两齿微露，似非佳相。一种缠绵之态，令人之意也消。

索观诗稿，有仅一联，或三四句，多未成篇者。询其故，笑曰："无师之作，愿得知己堪师者敲成之耳。"余戏题其签曰"锦囊佳句"，不知夭寿之机此已伏矣。

This was on the sixteenth of the seventh moon in the year 1775. In the winter of that year, one of my girl cousins, (the daughter of another maternal uncle of mine,) was going to get married and I again accompanied my mother to her maiden home.

Yün was the same age as myself, but ten months older, and as we had been accustomed to calling each other "elder sister" and "younger brother" from childhood, I continued to call her "Sister Su."

At this time the guests in the house all wore bright dresses, but Yün alone was clad in a dress of quiet colour, and had on a new pair of shoes. I noticed that the embroidery on her shoes was very fine, and learnt that it was her own work, so that I began to realize that she was gifted at other things, too, besides reading and writing.

Of a slender figure, she had drooping shoulders and a rather long neck, slim but not to the point of being skinny. Her eyebrows were arched and in her eyes there was a look of quick intelligence and soft refinement. The only defect was that her two front teeth were slightly inclined forward, which was not a mark of good omen. There was an air of tenderness about her which completely fascinated me.

I asked for the manuscripts of her poems and found that they consisted mainly of couplets and three or four lines, being unfinished poems, and I asked her the reason why. She smiled and said, "I have had no one to teach me poetry, and wish to have a good teacher-friend who could help me to finish these poems." I wrote playfully on the label of this book of poems the words: "Beautiful Lines in an Embroidered Case," and did not realize that in this case lay the cause of her short life.

　　是夜送亲城外，返，已漏三下，腹饥索饵，婢妪以枣脯进，余嫌其甜。芸暗牵余袖，随至其室，见藏有暖粥并小菜焉。余欣然举箸，忽闻芸堂兄玉衡呼曰："淑妹速来！"芸急闭门曰："已疲乏，将卧矣。"玉衡挤身而入，见余将吃粥，乃笑睨芸曰："顷我索粥，汝曰'尽矣'，乃藏此专待汝婿耶？"芸大窘避去，上下哗笑之。余亦负气，挈老仆先归。

　　自吃粥被嘲，再往，芸即避匿，余知其恐贻人笑也。

Chapter One, Wedded Bliss · 009

That night, when I came back from outside the city, whither I had accompanied my girl cousin the bride, it was already midnight, and I felt very hungry and asked for something to eat. A maid-servant gave me some dried dates, which were too sweet for me. Yün secretly pulled me by the sleeve into her room, and I saw that she had hidden away a bowl of warm congee and some dishes to go with it. I was beginning to take up the chopsticks and eat it with great gusto when Yün's boy cousin Yüheng called out, "Sister Su, come quick!" Yün quickly shut the door and said, "I am very tired and going to bed." Yüheng forced the door open and, seeing the situation, he said with a malicious smile at Yün, "So, that's it! A while ago I asked for congee and you said there was no more, but you really meant to keep it for your future husband." Yün was greatly embarrassed and everybody laughed at her, including the servants. On my part, I rushed away home with an old servant in a state of excitement.

Since the affair of the congee happened, she always avoided me when I went to her home, and I knew that she was only trying to avoid being made a subject of ridicule.

　　至乾隆庚子正月二十二日花烛之夕，见瘦怯身材依然如昔，头巾既揭，相视嫣然。合卺后，并肩夜膳，余暗于案下握其腕，暖尖滑腻，胸中不觉怦怦作跳。让之食，适逢斋期，已数年矣。暗计吃斋之初，正余出痘之期，因笑谓曰："今我光鲜无恙，姊可从此开戒否？"芸笑之以目，点之以首。

　　廿四日为余姊于归，廿三国忌不能作乐，故廿二之夜即为余姊款嫁，芸出堂陪宴。余在洞房与伴娘对酌，拇战辄北，大醉而卧；醒则芸正晓妆未竟也。

Our wedding took place on the twenty-second of the first moon in 1780. When she came to my home on that night, I found that she had the same slender figure as before. When her bridal veil was lifted, we looked at each other and smiled. After the drinking of the customary twin cups between bride and groom, we sat down together at dinner and I secretly held her hand under the table, which was warm and small, and my heart was palpitating. I asked her to eat and learnt that she was in her vegetarian fast, which she had been keeping for several years already. I found that the time when she began her fast coincided with my small-pox illness, and said to her laughingly, "Now that my face is clean and smooth without pock-marks, my dear sister, will you break your fast?" Yün looked at me with a smile and nodded her head.

As my own sister is going to get married on the twenty-fourth, only two days later, and as there was to be a national mourning and no music was to be allowed on the twenty-third, my sister was given a send-off dinner on the night of the twenty-second, my wedding day, and Yün was present at table. I was playing the finger-guessing game with the bride's companion in the bridal chamber and, being a loser all the time, I fell asleep drunk like a fish. When I woke up the next morning, Yün had not quite finished her morning toilet.

　　是日亲朋络绎，上灯后始作乐。廿四子正，余作新舅送嫁，丑末归来，业已灯残人静；悄然入室，伴妪盹于床下，芸卸妆尚未卧，高烧银烛，低垂粉颈，不知观何书而出神若此。因抚其肩曰："姊连日辛苦，何犹孜孜不倦耶？"

　　芸忙回首起立曰："顷正欲卧，开橱得此书，不觉阅之忘倦。西厢之名闻之熟矣，今始得见，真不愧才子之名，但未免形容尖薄耳。"

　　余笑曰："唯其才子，笔墨方能尖薄。"

　　伴妪在旁促卧，令其闭门先去。遂与比肩调笑，恍同密友重逢；戏探其怀，亦怦怦作跳，因俯其耳曰："姊何心春乃尔耶？"芸回眸微笑，便觉一缕情丝摇人魂魄；拥之入帐，不知东方之既白。

That day, we were kept busy entertaining guests and towards evening, music was played. After midnight, on the morning of the twenty-fourth, I, as the bride's brother, sent my sister away and came back towards three o'clock. The room was then pervaded with quietness, bathed in the silent glow of the candle-lights. I went in and saw Yün's bride's companion was taking a nap down in front of our bed on the floor, while Yün had taken off her bridal costume, but had not yet gone to bed. She was bending her beautiful white neck before the bright candles, quite absorbed reading a book. I patted her on the shoulder and said, "Sister, why are you still working so hard? You must be quite tired with the full days we've had."

Quickly Yün turned her head and stood up saying, "I was going to bed when I opened the book-case and saw this book and have not been able to leave it since. Now my sleepiness is all gone. I have heard of the name of *Western Chamber* for a long time, but today I see it for the first time. It is really the work of a genius, only I feel that its style is a little bit too biting."

"Only geniuses can write a biting style," I smiled and said.

The bride's companion asked us to go to bed, but we told her to shut the door and retire first. I began to sit down by Yün's side and we joked together like old friends after a long period of separation. I touched her breast in fun and felt that her heart was palpitating too. "Why is Sister's heart palpitating like that?" I bent down and whispered in her ear. Yün looked back at me with a smile and our souls were carried away in a mist of passion. Then we went to bed, when all too soon the dawn came.

　　芸作新妇，初甚缄默，终日无怒容，与之言，微笑而已。事上以敬，处下以和，井井然未尝稍失。每见朝暾上窗，即披衣急起，如有人呼促者然。余笑曰："今非吃粥比矣，何尚畏人嘲耶？"芸曰："曩之藏粥待君，传为话柄。今非畏嘲，恐堂上道新娘懒惰耳。"

　　余虽恋其卧而德其正，因亦随之早起。自此耳鬓相磨，亲同形影，爱恋之情有不可以言语形容者。

　　而欢娱易过，转睫弥月。时吾父稼夫公在会稽幕府，专役相迓，受业于武林赵省斋先生门下。先生循循善诱，余今日之尚能握管，先生力也。

Chapter

As a bride, Yün was very quiet at first. She was never sullen c displeased, and when people spoke to her, she merely smiled. She was respectful towards her superiors and kindly towards those under her. Whatever she did was done well, and it was difficult to find fault with her. When she saw the grey dawn shining in through the window, she would get up and dress herself as if she had been commanded to do so. "Why?" I asked, "You don't have to be afraid of gossip, like the days when you gave me that warm congee." "I was made a laughing-stock on account of that bowl of congee," she replied, "but now I am not afraid of people's talk; I only fear that our parents might think their daughter-in-law lazy."

Although I wanted her to lie in bed longer, I could not help admiring her virtue, and so got up myself, too, at the same time with her. And so every day we rubbed shoulders together and clung to each other like an object and its shadow, and the love between us was something that surpassed the language of words.

So the time passed happily and the honeymoon was too soon over. At this time, my father Chiafu was in the service of the Kueich'i district government, and he sent a special messenger to bring me there, for, it should be noted that, during this time, I was under the tutorship of Chao Shengtsai of Wulin [Hangchow]. Chao was a very kindly teacher and today the fact that I can write at all is due entirely to his credit.

　　归来完姻时，原订随侍到馆；闻信之余，心甚怅然，恐芸之对人堕泪，而芸反强颜劝勉，代整行装，是晚但觉神色稍异而已。临行，向余小语曰："无人调护，自去经心！"

　　及登舟解缆，正当桃李争妍之候，而余则恍同林鸟失群，天地异色。到馆后，吾父即渡江东去。

　　居三月，如十年之隔。芸虽时有书来，必两问一答，半多勉励词，余皆浮套语；心殊快快。每当风生竹院，月上蕉窗，对景怀人，梦魂颠倒。

　　先生知其情，即致书吾父，出十题而遣余暂归，喜同戍人得赦。

Now, when I came home for the wedding, it had been agreed that as soon as the ceremonies were over, I should go back at once to my father's place in order to resume my studies. So when I got this news, I did not know what to do. I was afraid Yün might break into tears, but on the other hand she tried to look cheerful and comforted me and urged me to go, and packed up things for me. Only that night I noticed that she did not look quite her usual self. At the time of parting, she whispered to me, "Take good care of yourself, for there will be no one to look after you."

When I went up on board the boat, I saw the peach and pear trees on the banks were in full bloom, but I felt like a lonely bird that had lost its companions and as if the world was going to collapse around me. As soon as I arrived, my father left the place and crossed the river for an eastward destination.

Thus three months passed, which seemed to me like ten insufferable long years. Although Yün wrote to me regularly, still for two letters that I sent her, I received only one in reply, and these letters contained only words of exhortation and the rest was filled with airy, conventional nothings, and I felt very unhappy. Whenever the breeze blew past my bamboo courtyard, or the moon shone upon my window behind the green banana leaves, I thought of her and was carried away into a region of dreams.

My teacher noticed this, and sent word to my father, saying that he would give me ten subjects for composition and let me go home. I felt like a garrison prisoner receiving his pardon.

　　登舟后，反觉一刻如年。及抵家，吾母处问安毕，入房，芸起相迎，握手未通片语，而两人魂魄恍恍然化烟成雾，觉耳中惺然一响，不知更有此身矣。

　　时当六月，内室炎蒸，幸居沧浪亭爱莲居西间壁，板桥内一轩临流，名曰我取，取"清斯濯缨，浊斯濯足"意也；檐前老树一株，浓阴覆窗，人面俱绿，隔岸游人往来不绝，此吾父稼夫公垂帘宴客处也。禀命吾母，携芸消夏于此，因暑罢绣，终日伴余课书论古，品月评花而已。芸不善饮，强之可三杯，教以射覆为令。自以为人间之乐无过于此矣。

Strange to say, when I got on to the boat and was on my way home, I felt that a quarter of an hour was like a long year. When I arrived home, I went to pay my respects to my mother and then entered my room. Yün stood up to welcome me, and we held each other's hands in silence, and it seemed then that our souls had melted away or evaporated like a mist. My ears tingled and I did not know where I was.

It was in the sixth moon, then, and the rooms were very hot. Luckily, we were next door to the Lotus Lover's Lodge of the Ts'anglang Pavilion on the east. Over the bridge, there was an open hall overlooking the water, called "After My Heart"—the reference was to an old poem: "When the water is clear, I will wash the tassels of my hat, and when the water is muddy, I will wash my feet." By the side of the eaves, there was an old tree which spread its green shade over the window, and made the people's faces look green with it; and across the creek, you could see people passing to and fro. This was where my father used to entertain his guests inside the bamboo-framed curtains.[1] I asked for permission from my mother to bring Yün and stay there for the summer. She stopped embroidery during the summer months because of the heat, and the whole day long, we were either reading together or discussing the ancient things, or else enjoying the moon and passing judgments on the flowers. Yün could not drink, but could take at most three cups when compelled to. I taught her literary games in which the loser had to drink. We thought there could not be a more happy life on earth than this.

---

[1] As there were no walls or lattices whatsoever round the pavilion, they used to hang down bamboo-framed curtains so that the dining party might not be seen by the people across the creek. — *Tr.*

　　一日，芸问曰："各种古文，宗何为是?"余曰："《国策》、《南华》取其灵快，匡衡、刘向取其雅健，史迁、班固取其博大，昌黎取其浑，柳州取其峭，庐陵取其宕，三苏取其辩，他若贾、董策对，庾、徐骈体，陆贽奏议，取资者不能尽举，在人之慧心领会耳。"

　　芸曰："古文全在识高气雄，女子学之恐难入彀；唯诗之一道，妾稍有领悟耳。"

　　余曰："唐以诗取士，而诗之宗匠必推李、杜。卿爱宗何人?"

　　芸发议曰："杜诗锤炼精纯，李诗潇洒落拓；与其学杜之森严，不如学李之活泼。"

　　余曰："工部为诗家之大成，学者多宗之，卿独取李，何也?"

　　芸曰："格律谨严，词旨老当，诚杜所独擅；但李诗宛如姑射仙子，有一种落花流水之趣，令人可爱。非杜亚于李，不过妾之私心宗杜心浅，爱李心深。"

One day Yün asked me, "Of all the ancient authors, which one should we regard as the master?" And I replied: *"Chankuots'eh* and Chuangtzǔ are noted for their agility of thought and expressiveness of style, K'uang Heng and Liu Hsiang are known for their classic severity, Ssuma Ch'ien and Pan Ku are known for their breadth of knowledge, Han Yü is known for his mellow qualities, Liu Tsungyüan for his rugged beauty, Ouyang Hsiu for his romantic abandon, and the Su's, father and sons, are known for their sustained eloquence. There are, besides, writings like the political essays of Chia Yi and Tung Chungshu, the euphuistic prose of Yü Hsin and Hsü Ling, the memorandums of Loh Chih, and others more than one can enumerate. True appreciation, however, must come from the reader himself."

"The ancient literature," Yün said, "depends for its appeal on depth of thought and greatness of spirit, which I am afraid it is difficult for a woman to attain. I believe, however, that I do understand something of poetry."

"Poetry was used," I said, "as a literary test in the imperial examinations of the T'ang Dynasty, and people acknowledge Li Po and Tu Fu as the master poets. Which of the two do you like better?"

"Tu's poems," she said, "are known for their workmanship and artistic refinement, while Li's poems are known for their freedom and naturalness of expression. I prefer the vivacity of Li Po to the severity of Tu Fu."

"Tu Fu is the acknowledged king of poets," said I, "and he is taken by most people as their model. Why do you prefer Li Po?"

"Of course," said she, "as for perfection of form and maturity of thought, Tu is the undisputed master, but Li Po's poems have the wayward charm of a nymph. His lines come naturally like dropping petals and flowing waters, and are so much lovelier for their spontaneity. I am not saying that Tu is second to Li; only personally I feel, not that I love Tu less, but that I love Li more."

余笑曰:"初不料陈淑珍乃李青莲知己。"

芸笑曰:"妾尚有启蒙师白乐天先生,时感于怀,未尝稍释。"

余曰:"何谓也?"

芸曰:"彼非作《琵琶行》者耶?"

余笑曰:"异哉!李太白是知己,白乐天是启蒙师,余适字三白为卿婿;卿与'白'字何其有缘耶?"

芸笑曰:"白字有缘,将来恐白字连篇耳。"(吴音呼"别字"为"白字"。)相与大笑。

余曰:"卿既知诗,亦当知赋之弃取?"

芸曰:"《楚辞》为赋之祖,妾学浅费解。就汉晋人中,调高语炼,似觉相如为最。"

余戏曰:"当日文君之从长卿,或不在琴而在此乎?"复相与大笑而罢。

"I say, I didn't know that you are a bosom friend of Li Po!"

"I have still in my heart another poet, Po Chüyi, who is my first tutor, as it were, and I have not been able to forget him."

"What do you mean?" I asked.

"Isn't he the one who wrote the poem on *The P'i P'a Player?*"

"This is very strange," I laughed and said. "So Li *Po* is your bosom friend, *Po* Chüyi is your first tutor and your husband's literary name is San *po*. It seems that your life is always bound up with the *Po's*."

"It is all right," Yün smiled and replied. "to have one's life bound up with the *Po's*, only I am afraid I shall be writing *Po* characters all my life." (For in Soochow we call misspelt words "*po* characters.") And we both laughed.

"Now that you know poetry," I said, "I should like also to know your taste for *fu* poems."

"The *Ch'u Tz'u* is, of course, the fountain head of *fu* poetry, but I find it difficult to understand. It seems to me that among the Han and Chin *fu* poets, Ssuma Hsiangju is the most sublime in point of style and diction."

"Perhaps," I said, "Wenchün was tempted to elope with Hsiangju not because of his *ch'in* music, but rather because of his *fu* poetry," and we laughed again.

　　余性爽直，落拓不羁，芸若腐儒，迂拘多礼，偶为披衣整袖，必连声道"得罪"，或递巾授扇，必起身来接。余始厌之，曰："卿欲以礼缚我耶？语曰，'礼多必诈'。"芸两颊发赤，曰："恭而有礼，何反言诈？"余曰："恭敬在心，不在虚文。"芸曰："至亲莫如父母，可内敬在心而外肆狂放耶？"余曰："前言戏之耳。"芸曰："世间反目多由戏起，后勿冤妾，令人郁死！"余乃挽之入怀，抚慰之，始解颜为笑。自此"岂敢"、"得罪"竟成语助词矣。鸿案相庄廿有三年，年愈久而情愈密。

I am by nature unconventional and straightforward, but Yün was a stickler for forms, like the Confucian schoolmasters. Whenever I put on a dress for her or tidied up her sleeves, she would say "So much obliged" again and again, and when I passed her a towel or a fan, she would always stand up to receive it. At first I disliked this and said to her, "Do you mean to tie me down with all this ceremony? There is a proverb which says, 'One who is overcourteous is crafty.'" Yün blushed all over and said, "I am merely trying to be polite and respectful, why do you charge me with craftiness?" "True respect is in the heart, and does not require such empty forms," said I, but Yün said, "There is no more intimate relationship than that between children and their parents. Do you mean to say that children should behave freely towards their parents and keep their respect only in their heart?" "Oh! I was only joking," I said. "The trouble is," said Yün, "most marital troubles begin with joking. Don't you accuse me of disrespect later, for then I shall die of grief without being able to defend myself." Then I held her close to my breast and caressed her until she smiled. From then on our conversations were full of "I'm sorry's" and "I beg your pardon's." And so we remained courteous to each other for twenty-three years of our married life like Liang Hung and Meng Kuang [of the Eastern Han Dynasty], and the longer we stayed together, the more passionately attached we became to each other.

　　家庭之内，或暗室相逢，窄途邂逅，必握手问曰："何处去？"私心怵怵，如恐旁人见之者。实则同行并坐，初犹避人，久则不以为意。芸或与人坐谈，见余至，必起立，偏挪其身，余就而并焉。彼此皆不觉其所以然者，始以为惭，继成不期然而然。独怪老年夫妇相视如仇者，不知何意。或曰："非如是，焉得白头偕老哉！"斯言诚然钦？

　　是年七夕，芸设香烛瓜果，同拜天孙于我取轩中。余镌"愿生生世世为夫妇"图章二方；余执朱文，芸执白文，以为往来书信之用。

Whenever we met each other in the house, whether it be in a dark room or in a narrow corridor, we used to hold each other's hands and ask, "Where are you going?" and we did this on the sly as if afraid that people might see us. As a matter of fact, we tried at first to avoid being seen sitting or walking together, but after a while, we did not mind it any more. When Yün was sitting and talking with somebody and saw me come, she would rise and move sideways for me to sit down together with her. All this was done naturally almost without any consciousness, and although at first we felt uneasy about it, later on it became a matter of habit. I cannot understand why all old couples must hate each other like enemies. Some people say, "If they weren't enemies, they would not be able to live together until old age." Well, I wonder!

On the seventh night of the seventh moon of that year, Yün prepared incense, candles and some melons and other fruits, so that we might together worship the Grandson of Heaven[1] in the Hall called "After My Heart." I had carved two seals with the inscription "That we might remain husband and wife from incarnation to incarnation." I kept the seal with positive characters, while she kept the one with negative characters, to be used in our correspondence.

[1] The seventh day of the seventh moon is the only day in the year when the pair of heavenly lovers, the Cowherd ("Grandson of Heaven") and the Spinster, are allowed to meet each other across the Milky Way. — *Tr.*

　　是夜月色颇佳，俯视河中，波光如练，轻罗小扇，并坐水窗，仰见飞云过天，变态万状。芸曰："宇宙之大，同此一月，不知今日世间，亦有如我两人之情兴否？"余曰："纳凉玩月，到处有之；若品论云霞，或求之幽闺绣闼，慧心默证者固亦不少；若夫妇同观，所品论者恐不在此云霞耳。"未几烛烬月沉，撤果归卧。

　　七月望，俗谓鬼节。芸备小酌，拟邀月畅饮。夜忽阴云如晦，芸怅然曰："妾能与君白头偕老，月轮当出。"余亦索然。但见隔岸萤光，明灭万点，梳织于柳堤蓼渚间。

That night, the moon was shining beautifully and when I looked down at the creek, the ripples shone like silvery chains. We were wearing light silk dresses and sitting together with a small fan in our hands, before the window overlooking the creek. Looking up at the sky, we saw the clouds sailing through the heavens, changing at every moment into a myriad forms, and Yün said, "This moon is common to the whole universe. I wonder if there is another pair of lovers quite as passionate as ourselves looking at the same moon tonight?" And I said, "Oh! there are plenty of people who will be sitting in the cool evening and looking at the moon, and perhaps also many women enjoying and appreciating the clouds in their chambers; but when a husband and wife are looking at the moon together, I hardly think that the clouds will form the subject of their conversation." By and by, the candle-lights went out, the moon sank in the sky, and we removed the fruits and went to bed.

The fifteenth of the seventh moon was All Souls' Day. Yün prepared a little dinner, so that we could drink together with the moon as our company, but when night came, the sky was suddenly overcast with dark clouds. Yün knitted her brow and said, "If it be the wish of God that we two should live together until there are silver threads in our hair, then the moon must come out again tonight." On my part I felt disheartened also. As we looked across the creek, we saw will-o'-the-wisps flitting in crowds hither and thither like ten thousand candle-lights, threading their way through the willows and smartweeds.

余与芸联句以遣闷怀，而两韵之后，逾联逾纵，想入非夷，随口乱道。芸已漱涎涕泪，笑倒余怀，不能成声矣。觉其鬓边茉莉浓香扑鼻，因拍其背，以他词解之曰："想古人以茉莉形色如珠，故供助妆压鬓，不知此花必沾油头粉面之气，其香更可爱，所供佛手当退三舍矣。"芸乃止笑曰："佛手乃香中君子，只在有意无意间；茉莉是香中小人，故须借人之势，其香也如胁肩谄笑。"余曰："卿何远君子而近小人？"芸曰："我笑君子爱小人耳。"

And then we began to compose a poem together, each saying two lines at a time, the first completing the couplet which the other had begun, and the second beginning another couplet for the other to finish, and after a few rhymes, the longer we kept on, the more nonsensical it became, until it was a jumble of slapdash doggerel. By this time, Yün was buried amidst tears and laughter and choking on my breast, while I felt the fragrance of the jasmine in her hair assail my nostrils. I patted her on the shoulder and said jokingly, "I thought that the jasmine was used for decoration in women's hair because it was clear and round like a pearl; I did not know that it is because its fragrance is so much finer when it is mixed with the smell of women's hair and powder. When it smells like that, even the citron cannot remotely compare with it." Then Yün stopped laughing and said, "The citron is the gentleman among the different fragrant plants because its fragrance is so slight that you can hardly detect it; on the other hand, the jasmine is a common fellow because it borrows its fragrance partly from others. Therefore, the fragrance of the jasmine is like that of a smiling sycophant." "Why, then," I said, "do you keep away from the gentleman and associate with the common fellow?" And Yün replied, "But I only laugh at that gentleman who loves a common fellow."

　　正话间，漏已三滴，渐见风扫云开，一轮涌出；乃大喜。倚窗对酌，酒未三杯，忽闻桥下哄然一声，如有人堕。就窗细瞩，波明如镜，不见一物，惟闻河滩有只鸭急奔声。余知沧浪亭畔素有溺鬼，恐芸胆怯，未敢即言。芸曰："噫！此声也，胡为乎来哉？"不禁毛骨皆栗，急闭窗，携酒归房。一灯如豆，罗帐低垂，弓影杯蛇，惊神未定。剔灯入帐，芸已寒热大作，余亦继之，困顿两旬；真所谓乐极灾生，亦是白头不终之兆。

While we were thus bandying words about, it was already mid-night, and we saw the wind had blown away the clouds in the sky and there appeared the full moon, round like a chariot wheel, and we were greatly delighted. And so we began to drink by the side of the window, but before we had tasted three cups, we heard suddenly the noise of a splash under the bridge, as if someone had fallen into the water. We looked out through the window and saw there was not a thing, for the water was as smooth as a mirror, except that we heard the noise of a duck scampering in the marshes. I knew that there was a ghost of someone who had been drowned by the side of the Ts'anglang Pavilion, but knowing that Yün was very timid, I dared not mention it to her. And Yün sighed and said, "Alas! Whence cometh this noise?" and we shuddered all over. Quickly we shut the window and carried the wine pot back into the room. The light of a rapeseed oil lamp was then burning as small as a pea, and the edges of the bed curtain hung low in the twilight, and we were shaking all over. We then made the lamplight a little brighter and went inside the bed curtain, and Yün already ran up a high fever. Soon I had a high temperature myself, and our illness dragged on for about twenty days. True it is that when the cup of happiness overflows, disaster follows, as the saying goes, and this was also an omen that we should not be able to live together until old age.

　　中秋日，余病初愈，以芸半年新妇，未尝一至间壁之沧浪亭，先令老仆约守者勿放闲人。于将晚时，偕芸及余幼妹，一妪一婢扶焉，老仆前导。过石桥，进门折东，曲径而入，叠石成山，林木葱翠。亭在土山之巅；循级至亭心，周望极目可数里，炊烟四起，晚霞灿然。隔岸名"近山林"，为大宪行台宴集之地，时正谊书院犹未启也。携一毯设亭中，席地环坐。守者烹茶以进。少焉，一轮明月已上林梢，渐觉风生袖底，月到波心，俗虑尘怀，爽然顿释。芸曰："今日之游乐矣。若驾一叶扁舟，往来亭下，不更快哉！"时已上灯，忆及七月十五夜之惊，相扶下亭而归。吴俗，妇女是晚不拘大家小户皆出，结队而游，名曰："走月亮"。沧浪亭幽雅清旷，反无一人至者。

On the fifteenth of the eighth moon, or the Mid-Autumn Festival, I had just recovered from my illness. Yün had now been a bride in my home for over half a year, but still had never been to the Ts'anglang Pavilion itself next door. So I first ordered an old servant to tell the watchman not to let any visitors enter the place. Toward evening, I went with Yün and my younger sister, supported by an amah and a maid-servant and led by an old attendant. We passed a bridge, entered a gate, turned eastwards and followed a zigzag path into the place, where we saw huge grottoes and abundant green trees. The Pavilion stood on the top of a hill. Going up by the steps to the top, one could look around for miles, where in the distance chimney smoke arose from the cottages against the background of clouds of rainbow hues. Over the bank, there was a grove called the "Forest by the Hill" where the high officials used to entertain their guests. Later on, the Chengyi College was erected on this spot, but it wasn't there yet. We brought a blanket which we spread on the Pavilion floor, and then sat round together, while the watchman served us tea. After a while, the moon had already arisen from behind the forest, and the breeze was playing about our sleeves, while the moon's image sparkled in the rippling water, and all worldly cares were banished from our breasts. "This is the end of a perfect day," said Yün. "Wouldn't it be fine if we could get a boat and row around the Pavilion!" At this time, the lights were already shining from people's homes, and thinking of the incident on the fifteenth night of the seventh moon, we left the Pavilion and hurried home. According to the custom at Soochow, the women of all families, rich or poor, came out in groups on the Mid-Autumn night, a custom which was called "pacing the moonlight." Strange to say, no one came to such a beautiful neighbourhood as the Ts'anglang Pavilion.

　　吾父稼夫公喜认义子，以故余异姓弟兄有二十六人；吾母亦有义
女九人。九人中王二姑、俞六姑与芸最和好。王痴憨善饮，俞豪爽善谈。
每集，必逐余居外，而得三女同榻；此俞六姑一人计也。余笑曰："俟
妹于归后，我当邀妹丈来，一住必十日。"俞曰："我亦来此，与嫂同榻，
不大妙耶？"芸与王微笑而已。

　　时为吾弟启堂娶妇，迁居饮马桥之仓米巷。屋虽宏畅，非复沧
浪亭之幽雅矣。吾母诞辰演剧，芸初以为奇观。吾父素无忌讳，点演
《惨别》等剧，老伶刻画，见者情动。余窥帘见芸忽起去，良久不出，
入内探之。俞与王亦继至。见芸一人支颐独坐镜奁之侧。余曰："何
不快乃尔？"芸曰："观剧原以陶情，今日之戏徒令人肠断耳。"俞与
王皆笑之。余曰："此深于情者也。"俞曰："嫂将竟日独坐于此耶？"
芸曰："俟有可观者再往耳。"王闻言先出，请吾母点《刺梁》、《后索》
等剧，劝芸出观，始称快。

My father Chiafu was very fond of adopting children; hence I had twenty-six adopted brothers. My mother, too, had nine adopted daughters, among whom Miss Wang, the second, and Miss Yü, the sixth, were Yün's best friends. Wang was a kind of a tomboy and a great drinker, while Yü was straightforward and very fond of talking. When they came together, they used to chase me out, so that the three of them could sleep in the same bed. I knew Miss Yü was responsible for this, and once I said to her in fun, "When you get married, I am going to invite your husband to come and keep him for ten days at a stretch." "I'll come here, too, then," said Miss Yü, "and sleep in the same bed with Yün. Won't that be fun?" At this Yün and Wang merely smiled.

At this time, my younger brother Ch'it'ang was going to get married, and we moved to Ts'angmi Alley by the Bridge of Drinking Horses. The house was quite big, but not so nice and secluded as the one by the Ts'anglang Pavilion. On the birthday of my mother, we had theatrical performances at home, and Yün at first thought them quite wonderful. Scorning all taboos, my father asked for the performance of a scene called "Sad Parting," and the actors played so realistically that the audience were quite touched. I noticed across the screen that Yün suddenly got up and disappeared inside for a long time. I went in to see her and the Misses Yü and Wang also followed suit. There I saw Yün sitting alone before her dressing table, resting her head on an arm. "Why are you so sad?" I asked. "One sees a play for diversion," Yün said, "but to-day's play only breaks my heart." Both Wang and Yü were laughing at her, but I defended her. "She is touched because hers is a profoundly emotional soul." "Are you going to sit here all day long?" asked Miss Yü. "I'll stay here until some better selection is being played," Yün replied. Hearing this, Miss Wang left first and asked my mother to select more cheerful plays like *Ch'ihliang and Househ*. Then Yün was persuaded to come out and watch the play, which made her happy again.

　　余堂伯父素存公早亡，无后，吾父以余嗣焉。墓在西跨塘福寿山祖茔之侧，每年春日必挈芸拜扫。王二姑闻其地有戈园之胜，请同往。芸见地下小乱石有苔纹，斑驳可观，指示余曰："以此叠盆山，较宣州白石为古致。"余曰："若此者恐难多得。"王曰："嫂果爱此，我为拾之。"即向守坟者借麻袋一，鹤步而拾之。每得一块，余曰"善"，即收之；余曰"否"，即去之。未几，粉汗盈盈，拽袋返曰："再拾则力不胜矣。"芸且拣且言曰："我闻山果收获，必藉猴力，果然！"王愤撮十指作哈痒状；余横阻之，责芸曰："人劳汝逸，犹作此语，无怪妹之动愤也。"

My uncle Such'ün died early without an heir, and my father made me succeed his line. His tomb was situated on the Hill of Good Fortune and Longevity in Hsikuat'ang by the side of our ancestral tombs, and I was accustomed to go there with Yün and visit the grave every spring. As there was a beautiful garden called Koyüan in its neighbourhood, Miss Wang begged to come with us. Yün saw that the pebbles on this hill had beautiful grains of different colours, and said to me, "If we were to collect these pebbles and make them into a grotto, it would be even more artistic than one made of Hsüanchow stones." I expressed the fear that there might not be enough of this kind. "If Yün really likes them, I'll pick them for her," said Miss Wang. So she borrowed a bag from the watchman, and went along with a stork's strides collecting them. Whenever she picked up one, she would ask for my opinion. If I said "good," she would put it into the bag; and if I said "no," she would throw it away. She stood up before long and came back to us with the bag, perspiring all over. "My strength will fail me if I am going to pick any more," she said. "I have been told," said Yün, as she was selecting the good ones in the bag, "that mountain fruits must be gathered with the help of monkeys, which seems quite true." Miss Wang was furious and stretched both her hands as if to tease her. I stopped her and said to Yün by way of reproof, "You cannot blame her for being angry, because she is doing all the work and you stand by and say such unkind things."

　　归途游戈园，稚绿娇红，争妍竞媚。王素憨，逢花必折。芸叱曰："既无瓶养，又不簪戴，多折何为！"王曰："不知痛痒者，何害？"余笑曰："将来罚嫁麻面多须郎，为花泄忿。"王怒余以目，掷花于地，以莲钩拨入池中，曰："何欺侮我之甚也！"芸笑解之而罢。

　　芸初缄默，喜听余议论。余调其言，如蟋蟀之用纤草，渐能发议。其每日饭必用茶泡，喜食芥卤乳腐，吴俗呼为"臭乳腐"；又喜食虾卤瓜。此二物余生平所最恶者，因戏之曰："狗无胃而食粪，以其不知臭秽；蜣螂团粪而化蝉，以其欲修高举也。卿其狗耶，蝉耶？"芸曰："腐取其价廉而可粥可饭，幼时食惯。今至君家，已如蜣螂化蝉，犹喜食之者，不忘本出。至卤瓜之味，到此初尝耳。"

Then on our way back, we visited the Koyüan Garden, in which we saw a profusion of flowers of all colours. Wang was very childish; she would now and then pick a flower for no reason, and Yün scolded her, saying, "What do you pick so many flowers for, since you are not going to put them in a vase or in your hair?" "Oh! what's the harm? These flowers don't feel anything." "All right," I said, "you will be punished for this one day by marrying a pock-marked bearded fellow for your husband to avenge the flowers." Wang looked at me in anger, threw the flowers to the ground and kicked them into the pond. "Why do you all bully me?" she said. However, Yün made it up with her, and she was finally pacified.

Yün was at first very quiet and loved to hear me talk, but I gradually taught her the art of conversation as one leads a cricket with a blade of grass. She then gradually learnt the art of conversation. For instance, at meals, she always mixed her rice with tea, and loved to eat stale picked bean-curd, called "stinking bean-curd" in Soochow. Another thing she liked to eat was a kind of small pickled cucumber. I hated both of these things, and said to her in fun one day, "The dog, which has no stomach, eats human refuse because it doesn't know that refuse stinks, while the beetle rolls in dunghills and is changed into a cicada because it wants to fly up to heaven. Now are you a dog or a beetle?" To this Yün replied, "One eats beancurd because it is so cheap and it goes with dry rice as well as with congee. I am used to this from childhood. Now I am married into your home, like a beetle that has been transformed into a cicada, but I am still eating it because one should not forget old friends. As for pickled cucumber, I tasted it for the first time in your home."

　　余曰："然则我家系狗窦耶？"芸窘而强解曰："夫粪，人家皆有之，
要在食与不食之别耳。然君喜食蒜，妾亦强啖之。腐不敢强，瓜可掩
鼻略尝，入咽当知其美；此犹无盐貌丑而德美也。"余笑曰："卿陷我
作狗耶？"芸曰："妾作狗久矣，屈君试尝之。"以箸强塞余口，余掩
鼻咀嚼之，似觉脆美；开鼻再嚼，竟成异味。从此亦喜食。芸以麻油
加白糖少许拌卤腐，亦鲜美。以卤瓜捣烂拌卤腐，名之曰"双鲜酱"，
有异味。余曰："始恶而终好之，理之不可解也。"芸曰："情之所钟，
虽丑不嫌。"

"Oh, then, my home is a dog's kennel, isn't it?" Yün was embarrassed and tried to explain it away by saying, "Of course there is refuse in every home; the only difference is whether one eats it or not. You yourself eat garlic, for instance, and I have tried to eat it with you. I won't compel you to eat stinking bean-curd, but cucumber is really very nice, if you hold your breath while eating. You will see when you have tasted it yourself. It is like Wuyien, an ugly but virtuous woman of old." "Are you going to make me a dog?" I asked. "Well, I have been a dog for a long time, why don't you try to be one?" So she picked a piece of cucumber with her chopsticks and stuck it into my mouth. I held my breath and ate it and found it indeed delicious. Then I ate it in the usual way and found it to have a marvellous flavour. And from that time on, I loved the cucumber also. Yün also prepared pickled bean-curd mixed with sesame seed oil and sugar, which I found also to be a delicacy. We then mixed pickled cucumber with pickled bean-curd and called the mixture "the double-flavoured gravy." I said I could not understand why I disliked it at first and began to love it so now. "If you are in love with a thing, you will forget its ugliness," said Yün.

　　余启堂弟妇，王虚舟先生孙女也，催妆时偶缺珠花。芸出其纳采所受者呈吾母，婢妪旁惜之。芸曰："凡为妇人，已属纯阴，珠乃纯阴之精，用为首饰，阳气全克矣，何贵焉？"而于破书残画，反极珍惜。书之残缺不全者，必搜集分门，汇订成帙，统名之曰"断简残编"；字画之破损者，必觅故纸粘补成幅，有破缺处，倩予全好而卷之，名曰"弃余集赏"。于女红、中馈之暇，终日琐琐，不惮烦倦。芸于破簏烂卷中，偶获片纸可观者，如得异宝。旧邻冯妪每收乱卷卖之。其癖好与余同，且能察眼意，懂眉语，一举一动，示之以色，无不头头是道。

My younger brother Ch'it'ang married the grand-daughter of Wang Hsüchou. It happened that on the wedding day, she wanted some pearls. Yün took her own pearls, which she had received as her bridal gift, and gave them to my mother. The maid-servant thought it a pity, but Yün said, "A woman is an incarnation of the female principle, and so are pearls. For a woman to wear pearls would be to leave no room for the male principle. For that reason I don't prize them." She had, however, a peculiar fondness for old books and broken slips of painting. Whenever she saw odd volumes of books, she would try to sort them out, arrange them in order, and have them rebound properly. These were collected and labelled "Ancient Relics." When she saw scrolls of calligraphy or painting that were partly spoilt, she would find some old paper and paste them up nicely, and ask me to fill up the broken spaces.[1] These were kept rolled up properly and called "Beautiful Gleanings." This was what she was busy about the whole day when she was not attending to the kitchen or needlework. When she found in old trunks or piles of musty volumes any writing or painting that pleased her, she felt as if she had discovered some precious relic, and an old woman neighbour of ours, by the name of Feng, used to buy up old scraps and sell them to her. She had the same tastes and habits as myself, and besides had the talent of reading my wishes by a mere glance or movement of the eyebrow, doing things without being told and doing them to my perfect satisfaction.

[1] The author was a painter, and for a time painted for his living. — *Tr.*

　　余尝曰："惜卿雌而伏，苟能化女为男，相与访名山，搜胜迹，遨游天下，不亦快哉！"

　　芸曰："此何难。俟妾鬓斑之后，虽不能远游五岳，而近地之虎阜、灵岩，南至西湖，北至平山，尽可偕游。"

　　余曰："恐卿鬓斑之日，步履已艰。"

　　芸曰："今世不能，期以来世。"

　　余曰："来世卿当作男，我为女子相从。"

　　芸曰："必得不昧今生，方觉有情趣。"

　　余笑曰："幼时一粥犹谈不了；若来世不昧今生，合卺之夕，细谈隔世，更无合眼时矣。"

Once I said to her, "It is a pity that you were born a woman. If you were a man, we could travel together and visit all the great mountains and the famous places throughout the country."

"Oh! this is not so very difficult," said Yün. "Wait till I have got my grey hairs. Even if I cannot accompany you to the Five Sacred Mountains[1] then, we can travel to the nearer places, like Huch'iu and Lingyen, as far south as the West Lake and as far north as P'ingshan [in Yangchow]."

"Of course this is all right, except that I am afraid when you are grey-haired, you will be too old to travel."

"If I can't do it in this life, then I shall do it in the next."

"In the next life, you must be born a man and I will be your wife."

"It will be quite beautiful if we can then still remember what has happened in this life."

"That's all very well, but even a bowl of congee has provided material for so much conversation. We shan't be able to sleep a wink the whole wedding night, but shall be discussing what we have done in the previous existence, if we can still remember what's happened in this life then."

[1] The Five Sacred Mountains are: (1) Taishan, the East Sacred Mountains (in Shantung), (2) Huashan, the West Sacred Mountain (in Shensi), (3) Hengshan, the North Sacred Mountain (in Shansi), (4) Hengshan, the South Sacred Mountain (in Hunan) and (5) Sungshan the Central Sacred Mountain (in Honan). — *Tr.*

　　芸曰："世传月下老人专司人间婚姻事，今生夫妇已承牵合，来世姻缘亦须仰藉神力，盍绘一像祀之？"

　　时有苕溪戚柳堤，名遵，善写人物，倩绘一像，一手挽红丝，一手携杖悬姻缘簿，童颜鹤发，奔驰于非烟非雾中；此戚君得意笔也。友人石琢堂为题赞语于首，悬之内室。每逢朔望，余夫妇必焚香拜祷。后因家庭多故，此画竟失所在，不知落在谁家矣。"他生未卜此生休"，两人痴情，果邀神鉴耶？

"It is said that the Old Man under the Moon is in charge of matrimony," said Yün. "He was good enough to make us husband and wife in this life, and we shall still depend on his favour in the affair of marriage in the next incarnation. Why don't we make a painting of him and worship him in our home?"

So we asked a Mr. Ch'i Liut'i of T'iaoch'i who specialized in portraiture, to make a painting of the Old Man under the Moon, which he did. It was a picture of the Old Man holding, in one hand, a red silk thread [for the purpose of binding together the hearts of all couples] and, in the other, a walking-stick with the Book of Matrimony suspended from it. He had white hair and a ruddy complexion, apparently bustling about in a cloudy region. Altogether it was a very excellent painting of Ch'i's. My friend Shih Chot'ang wrote some words of praise on it and we hung the picture in our chamber. On the first and fifteenth of every month, we burnt incense and prayed together before him. I do not know where this picture is now, as we have lost it after all the changes and upsets in our family life. "Ended is the present life and uncertain the next," as the poet says. I wonder if God will listen to the prayer of us two silly lovers.

　　迁仓米巷，余颜其卧楼曰"宾香阁"，盖以芸名而取如宾意也。院窄墙高，一无可取。后有厢楼，通藏书处，开窗对陆氏废园，但有荒凉之象。沧浪风景，时切芸怀。

　　有老妪居金母桥之东，埂巷之北。绕屋皆菜圃，编篱为门。门外有池约亩许，花光树影，错杂篱边。其地即元末张士诚王府废基也。屋西数武，瓦砾堆成土山，登其巅可远眺，地旷人稀，颇饶野趣。

After we had moved to Ts'angmi Alley, I called our bedroom the "Tower of My Guest's Fragrance," with a reference to Yün's name,[1] and to the story of Liang Hung and Meng Kuang who, as husband and wife, were always courteous to each other "like guests." We rather disliked the house because the walls were too high and the courtyard was too small. At the back, there was another house, leading to the library. Looking out of the window at the back, one could see the old garden of Mr. Loh then in a dilapidated condition. Yün's thoughts still hovered about the beautiful scenery of the T'sanglang Pavilion.

At this time, there was an old peasant woman living on the east of Mother Gold's Bridge and the north of Kenghsiang. Her little cottage was surrounded on all sides by vegetable fields and had a wicker gate. Outside the gate, there was a pond about thirty yards across, and a wilderness of flowers and trees covered the sides of the hedgerow. This was the old site of the home of Chang Ssŭch'eng at the end of the Yüan Dynasty. A few paces to the west of the cottage, there was a mound filled with broken bricks, from the top of which one could command a view of the surrounding territory, which was an open country with a stretch of wild vegetation.

[1] "Yün" in Chinese means a fragrant weed — *Tr.*

　　妪偶言及，芸神往不置，谓余曰："自别沧浪，梦魂常绕，今不得已而思其次，其老妪之居乎？"余曰："连朝秋暑灼人，正思得一清凉地以消长昼。卿若愿往，我先观其家，可居，即袱被而往，作一月盘桓何如？"芸曰："恐堂上不许。"余曰："我自请之。"越日至其地，屋仅二间，前后隔而为四，纸窗竹榻，颇有幽趣。老妪知余意，欣然出其卧室为赁，四壁糊以白纸，顿觉改观。于是禀知吾母，挈芸居焉。

　　邻仅老夫妇二人，灌园为业，知余夫妇避暑于此，先来通殷勤，并钓池鱼，摘园蔬为馈。偿其价，不受，芸作鞋报之，始谢而受。

Once the old woman happened to mention the place, and Yün kept on thinking about it. So she said to me one day, "Since leaving the Ts'anglang Pavilion, I have been dreaming about it all the time. As we cannot live there, we must put up with the second best. I have a great idea to go and live in the old woman's cottage." "I have been thinking, too," I said, "of a place to go to and spend the long summer days. If you think you'll like the place, I'll go ahead and take a look. If it is satisfactory, we can carry our beddings along and go and stay there for a month. How about it?" "I'm afraid mother won't allow us." "Oh! I'll see to that," I told her. So the next day, I went there and found that the cottage consisted only of two rooms, which were partitioned into four. With paper windows and bamboo beds, the house would be quite a delightfully cool place to stay in. The old woman knew what I wanted and gladly rented me her bedroom, which then looked quite new, when I had repapered the walls. I then informed my mother of it and went to stay there with Yün.

Our only neighbours were an old couple who raised vegetables for the market. They knew that we were going to stay there for the summer, and came and called on us, bringing us some fish from the pond and vegetables from their own fields. We offered to pay for them, but they wouldn't take any money, and afterwards Yün made a pair of shoes for each of them, which they were finally persuaded to accept.

　　时方七月，绿树阴浓，水面风来，蝉鸣聒耳。邻老又为制鱼竿，
与芸垂钓于柳阴深处。日落时，登土山，观晚霞夕照，随意联吟，有"兽
云吞落日，弓月弹流星"之句。少焉，月印池中，虫声四起，设竹榻
于篱下。老妪报酒温饭熟，遂就月光对酌，微醺而饭。浴罢则凉鞋蕉扇，
或坐或卧，听邻老谈因果报应事。三鼓归卧，周体清凉，几不知身
居城市矣。

　　篱边倩邻老购菊，遍植之。九月花开，又与芸居十日。吾母亦欣
然来观，持螯对菊，赏玩竟日。

This was in the seventh moon when the trees cast a green shade over the place. The summer breeze blew over the water of the pond, and cicadas filled the air with their singing the whole day. Our old neighbour also made a fishing rod for us, and we used to angle together under the shade of the willow trees. Late in the afternoons, we would go up on the mound to have a look at the evening glow and compose lines of poetry, when we felt so inclined. Two of the best lines were:

"Beast-clouds swallow the sinking sun,
And the bow-moon shoots the falling stars."

After a while, the moon cut her image in the water, insects began to chirp all round, and we placed a bamboo bed near the hedgerow to sit or lie upon. The old woman then would inform us that wine had been warmed up and dinner prepared, and we would sit down to have a little drink under the moon before our meal. Then after bath, we would put on our slippers and carry a fan, and lie or sit there, listening to old tales of retribution told by our neighbour. When we came in to sleep about midnight, we felt nice and cool all over the body, almost forgetting that we were living in a city.

There along the hedgerow, we asked the gardener to plant chrysanthemums. The flowers bloomed in the ninth moon, and we continued to stay there for another ten days. My mother was also quite delighted and came to see us there. So we ate crabs in the midst of chrysanthemums and whiled away the whole day.

　　芸喜曰："他年当与君卜筑于此，买绕屋菜园十亩，课仆妪，植瓜蔬，以供薪水。君画我绣，以为诗酒之需。布衣菜饭，可乐终身，不必作远游计也。"余深然之。今即得有境地，而知己沦亡，可胜浩叹！

　　离余家半里许，醋库巷有洞庭君祠，俗呼水仙庙，回廊曲折，小有园亭。每逢神诞，众姓各认一落，密悬一式之玻璃灯，中设宝座，旁列瓶几，插花陈设，以较胜负。日惟演戏，夜则参差高下，插烛于瓶花间，名曰"花照"。花光灯影，宝鼎香浮，若龙宫夜宴。司事者或笙箫歌唱，或煮茗清谈，观者如蚁集，檐下皆设栏为限。

Yün was quite enchanted with all this and said, "Some day we must build a cottage here. We'll buy ten *mow* of ground around the cottage, and see to our servants planting in the fields vegetables and melons to be sold for the expenses of our daily meals. You will paint and I will do embroidery, from which we could make enough money to buy wine for entertaining our friends who will gather here together to compose poems. Thus, clad in simple gowns and eating simple meals, we could live a very happy life together without going anywhere." I fully agreed with her. Now the place is still there, while my bosom friend is dead. Alas! such is life!

About half a *li* from my home, there was a temple to the God of the Tung-t'ing Lake, popularly known as the Narcissus Temple, situated in the Ch'uk'u Alley. It had many winding corridors and something of a garden with pavilions. On the birthday of the God, every clan would be assigned a corner in the Temple, where they would hang beautiful glass lanterns of a kind, with a chair in the center, on the either side of which were placed vases on wooden stands. These vases were decorated with flowers for competition. In the daytime, there would be theatrical performances, while at night the flower-vases were brilliantly illuminated with candlelights in their midst, a custom which was called "Illuminated Flowers." With the flowers and the lanterns and the smell of incense, the whole show resembled a night feast in the Palace of the Dragon King. The people there would sing or play music, or gossip over their tea-cups. The audience stood around in crowds to look at the show and there was a railing at the curb to keep them within a certain limit.

　　余为众友邀去插花布置，因得躬逢其盛。归家向芸艳称之。芸曰："惜
妾非男子，不能往。"余曰："冠我冠，衣我衣，亦化女为男之法也。"
于是易髻为辫，添扫蛾眉，加余冠，微露两鬓，尚可掩饰。服余衣长
一寸又半，于腰间折而缝之，外加马褂。芸曰："脚下将奈何？"余曰："坊
间有蝴蝶履，小大由之，购亦极易，且早晚可代撒鞋之用，不亦善乎？"
芸欣然。及晚餐后，装束既毕，效男子拱手阔步者良久，忽变卦曰："妾
不去矣。为人识出既不便，堂上闻之又不可。"余怂恿曰："庙中司事
者谁不知我，即识出亦不过付之一笑耳。吾母现在九妹丈家，密去密来，
焉得知之。"

I was asked by my friends to help in the decorations and so had the pleasure of taking part in it. When Yün heard me speaking about it at home, she remarked, "It is a pity that I am not a man and cannot go to see it." "Why, you could put on my cap and gown and disguise yourself as a man," I suggested. Accordingly she changed her coiffure into a queue, painted her eyebrows, and put on my cap. Although her hair showed slightly round the temples, it passed off tolerably well. As my gown was found to be an inch and a half too long, she tucked it round the waist and put on a *makua* on top. "What am I going to do about my feet?" she asked. I told her there was a kind of shoes called "butterfly shoes," which could fit any size of feet and were very easy to obtain at the shops, and suggested buying a pair for her, which she could also use as slippers later on at home. Yün was delighted with the idea, and after supper, when she had finished her make-up, she paced about the room, imitating the gestures and gait of a man for a long time, when all of a sudden she changed her mind and said, "I am not going! It would be so embarrassing if somebody should discover it, and besides, our parents would object." Still I urged her to go. "Who doesn't know me at the Temple?" I said. "Even if they should find it out, they would laugh it off as a joke. Mother is at present in the home of the ninth sister. We could steal away and back without letting anyone know about it."

　　芸揽镜自照，狂笑不已。余强挽之，悄然径去。遍游庙中，无识
出女子者，或问何人，以表弟对，拱手而已。最后至一处，有少妇幼
女坐于所设宝座后，乃杨姓司事者之眷属也。芸忽趋彼通款曲，身一
侧，而不觉一按少妇之肩。旁有婢媪怒而起曰："何物狂生，不法乃尔！"
余欲为措词掩饰。芸见势恶，即脱帽翘足示之曰："我亦女子耳。"相
与愕然，转怒为欢。留茶点，唤肩舆送归。

　　吴江钱师竹病故，吾父信归，命余往吊。芸私谓余曰："吴江必
经太湖，妾欲偕往，一宽眼界。"余曰："正虑独行踽踽，得卿同行固妙，
但无可托词耳。"

Yün then had such fun looking at herself in the mirror. I dragged her along and we stole away together to the Temple. For a long time nobody in the Temple could detect it. When people asked, I simply said she was my boy cousin, and people would merely curtsy with their hands together and pass on. Finally, we came to a place where there were some young women and girls sitting behind the flower show. They were the family of the owner of that show, by the name of Yang. Yün suddenly went over to talk with them, and while talking, she casually leant over and touched the shoulder of a young woman. The maid-servants nearby shouted angrily, "How dare the rascal!" I attempted to explain and smooth the matter over, but the servants still scowled ominously on us, and seeing that the situation was desperate, Yün took off her cap and showed her feet, saying "Look here, I am a woman, too!" They all stared at each other in surprise, and then, instead of being angry, began to laugh. We were then asked to sit down and have some tea. Soon afterwards we got sedan-chairs and came home.

When Mr. Ch'ien Shihchu of Wukiang died of an illness, my father wrote a letter to me, asking me to go and attend the funeral. Yün secretly expressed her desire to come along since on our way to Wukiang, we would pass the Taihu Lake, which she wished very much to see. I told her that I was just thinking it would be too lonely for me to go alone, and that it would be excellent, indeed, if she could come along, except that I could not think of a pretext for her going.

　　芸曰："托言归宁。君先登舟，妾当继至。"余曰："若然，归途当泊舟万年桥下，与卿待月乘凉，以续沧浪韵事。"

　　时六月十八日也。是日早凉，携一仆先至胥江渡口，登舟而待。芸果肩舆至，解维出虎啸桥，渐见风帆沙鸟，水天一色。芸曰："此即所谓太湖耶？今得见天地之宽，不虚此生矣。想闺中人有终身不能见此者。"闲话未几，风摇岸柳，已抵江城。

　　余登岸拜奠毕，归视舟中洞然，急询舟子。舟子指曰："不见长桥柳阴下观鱼鹰捕鱼者乎？"盖芸已与船家女登岸矣。余至其后，芸犹粉汗盈盈，倚女而出神焉。余拍其肩曰："罗衫汗透矣！"芸回首曰："恐钱家有人到舟，故暂避之。君何回来之速也？"余笑曰："欲捕逃耳。"

"Oh, I could say that I am going to see my mother," Yün said. "You can go ahead, and I shall come along to meet you." "If so," I said, "we can tie up our boat beneath the Bridge of Ten Thousand Years on our way home, where we shall be able to look at the moon again as we did at the Ts'anglang Pavilion."

This was on the eighteenth day of the sixth moon. That day, I brought a servant and arrived first at Hsükiang Ferry, where I waited for her in the boat. By and by, Yün arrived in a sedan-chair, and we started off, passing by the Tiger's Roar Bridge, where the view opened up and we saw sailing boats and sand-birds flitting over the lake. The water was a white stretch, joining the sky at the horizon. "So this is Taihu!" Yün exclaimed. "I know now how big the universe is, and I have not lived in vain! I think a good many ladies never see such a view in their whole lifetime." As we were occupied in conversation, it wasn't very long before we saw swaying willows on the banks, and we knew we had arrived at Wukiang.

I went up to attend the funeral ceremony, but when I came back, Yün was not in the boat. I asked the boatman and he said, "Don't you see someone under the willow trees by the bridge, watching the cormorants catching fish?" Yün, then, had gone up with the boatman's daughter. When I got behind her, I saw that she was perspiring all over, still leaning on the boatman's daughter and standing there absorbed looking at the cormorants. I patted her shoulder and said, "You are wet through." Yün turned her head and said, "I was afraid that your friend Ch'ien might come to the boat, so I left to avoid him. Why did you come back so early?" "In order to catch the renegade!" I replied.

　　于是相挽登舟，返棹至万年桥下，阳乌犹未落山。舟窗尽落，清风徐来，纨扇罗衫，剖瓜解暑。少焉霞映桥红，烟笼柳暗，银蟾欲上，渔火满江矣。命仆至船梢与舟子同饮。

　　船家女名素云，与余有杯酒交，人颇不俗。招之与芸同坐。船头不张灯火，待月快酌，射覆为令。素云双目闪闪，听良久，曰："筋政侬颇娴习。从未闻有斯令，愿受教。"芸即譬其言而开导之，终茫然。

We then came back hand-in-hand to the boat, and when we stopped at the Bridge of Ten Thousand Years. The sun had not yet gone down. And we let down all the windows to allow the river breeze to come in, and there, dressed in light silk and holding a silk fan, we sliced a melon to cool ourselves. Soon the evening glow was casting a red hue over the bridge, and the distant haze enveloped the willow trees in twilight. The moon was then coming up, and all along the river we saw a stretch of lights coming from the fishing boats. I asked my servant to go astern and have a drink with the boatman.

The boatman's daughter was called Suyün. She was quite a likeable girl, and I had known her before. I beckoned her to come and sit together with Yün on the bow of the boat. We did not put on any light, so that we could the better enjoy the moon, and there we sat drinking heartily and playing literary games with wine as forfeit. Suyün just stared at us, listening for a long time before she said, "Now I am quite familiar with all sorts of wine-games, but have never heard of this one. Will you explain it to me?" Yün tried to explain it by all sorts of analogies to her, but still she failed to understand.

　　余笑曰：“女先生且罢论。我有一言作譬，即了然矣。”芸曰：“君
若何譬之？”余曰：“鹤善舞而不能耕，牛善耕而不能舞，物性然也。
先生欲反而教之，无乃劳乎？”素云笑捶余肩曰：“汝骂我耶？”芸出
令曰：“只许动口，不许动手！违者罚大觥。”素云量豪，满斟一觥，
一吸而尽。余曰：“动手但准摸索，不准捶人。”芸笑挽素云置余怀，
曰：“请君摸索畅怀。”余笑曰：“卿非解人，摸索在有意无意间耳。拥而
狂探，田舍郎之所为也。”时四鬓所簪茉莉，为酒气所蒸，杂以粉汗
油香，芳馨透鼻。余戏曰：“小人臭味充满船头，令人作恶。”素云不
禁握拳连捶曰：“谁教汝狂嗅耶？”

Then I laughed and said, "Will the lady teacher please stop a moment? I have a parable for explaining it, and she will understand at once." "You try it, then!" "The stork," I said, "can dance, but cannot plow, while the buffalo can plow, but cannot dance. That lies in the nature of things. You are making a fool of yourself by trying to teach the impossible to her." Suyün pummelled my shoulder playfully, saying, "You are speaking of me as a buffalo, aren't you?" Then Yün said, "Hereafter let's make a rule: let's have it out with our mouths, but no hands! One who breaks the rule will have to drink a big cup." As Suyün was a great drinker, she filled a cup full and drank it up at a draught. "I suggest that one may be allowed to use one's hands for caressing, but not for striking," I said. Yün then playfully pushed Suyün into my lap, saying, "Now you can caress her to your full." "How stupid of you!" I laughed in reply. "The beauty of caressing lies in doing it naturally and half unconsciously. Only a country bumpkin will hug and caress a woman roughly." I noticed that the jasmine in the hair of both of them gave out a strange fragrance, mixed with the flavour of wine, powder and hair lotion and remarked to Yün, "The 'common little fellow' stinks all over the place. It makes me sick." Hearing this, Suyün struck me blow after blow with her fist in a rage, saying, "Who told you to smell it?"

芸呼曰："违令，罚两大觥！"

素云曰："彼又以小人骂我，不应捶耶？"

芸曰："彼之所谓小人，盖有故也。请干此，当告汝。"

素云乃连尽两觥。芸乃告以沧浪旧居乘凉事。

素云曰："若然，真错怪矣。当再罚。"又干一觥。

芸曰："久闻素娘善歌，可一聆妙音否？"素即以象箸击小碟而歌。

芸欣然畅饮，不觉酩酊，乃乘舆先归。余又与素云茶话片刻，步月而回。

"She breaks the rule! Two big cups!" Yün shouted.

"He called me 'common little fellow.' Why shouldn't I strike him?" protested Suyün.

"He really means by the 'common little fellow' something which you don't understand. You finish these two cups first and I'll tell you."

When Suyün had finished the two cups, Yün told her of our discussion about the jasmine at the Ts'anglang Pavilion.

"Then the mistake is mine. I must be penalized again," said Suyün. And she drank a third cup.

Yün said then that she had long heard of her reputation as a singer and would like to hear her sing. This Suyün did beautifully, beating time with her ivory chopsticks on a little plate. Yün drank merrily until she was quite drunk, when she took a sedan-chair and went home first, while I remained chatting with Suyün for a moment, and then walked home under the moonlight.

　　时余寄居友人鲁半舫家萧爽楼中。越数日，鲁夫人误有所闻，私告芸曰："前日闻若婿挟两妓饮于万年桥舟中，子知之否？"芸曰："有之，其一即我也。"因以偕游始末详告之。鲁大笑，释然而去。

　　乾隆甲寅七月，余自粤东归，有同伴携妾回者，曰徐秀峰，余之表妹婿也，艳称新人之美，邀芸往观。芸他日谓秀峰曰："美则美矣，韵犹未也。"秀峰曰："然则若郎纳妾，必美而韵者乎？"芸："然。"从此痴心物色，而短于资。

At this time, we were staying in the home of our friend Lu Panfang, in a house called Hsiaoshuanglou. A few days afterwards, Mrs. Lu heard of the story from someone, and secretly told Yün, "Do you know that your husband was drinking a few days ago at the Bridge of Ten Thousand Years with two sing-song girls?" "Yes, I do," replied Yün, "and one of the sing-song girls was myself." Then she told her the whole story and Mrs. Lu had a good laugh at herself.

When I came back from Eastern Kwangtung in the seventh moon, 1794, there was a boy cousin-in-law of mine, by the name of Hsü Hsiufeng, who had brought home with him a concubine. He was crazy about her beauty and asked Yün to go and see her. After seeing her, Yün remarked to Hsiufeng one day, "She has beauty but no charm." "Do you mean to say that when your husband takes a concubine, she must have both beauty and charm?" answered Hsiufeng. Yün replied in the affirmative. So from that time on, she was quite bent on finding a concubine for me, but was short of cash.

　　时有浙妓温冷香者，寓于吴，有咏柳絮四律，沸传吴下，好事者多和之。余友吴江张闲憨素赏冷香，携柳絮诗索和。芸微其人而置之；余技痒而和其韵，中有"触我春愁偏婉转，撩他离绪更缠绵"之句，芸甚击节。

　　明年乙卯秋八月五日，吾母将挈芸游虎丘，闲憨忽至，曰："余亦有虎丘之游。今日特邀君作探花使者。"因请吾母先行，期于虎丘半塘相晤。拉余至冷香寓，见冷香已半老，有女名憨园，瓜期未破，亭亭玉立，真"一泓秋水照人寒"者也。款接间，颇知文墨。有妹文园，尚雏。

At this time there was a Chekiang sing-song girl by the name of Wen Lenghsiang, who was staying at Soochow. She had composed four poems on the Willow Catkins which were talked about all over the city, and many scholars wrote poems in reply, using the same rhyme-words as her originals, as was the custom. There was a friend of mine, Chang Hsienhan of Wukiang, who was a good friend of Lenghsiang and brought her poems to me, asking us to write some in reply. Yün wasn't interested because she did not think much of her, but I was intrigued and composed one on the flying willow catkins which filled the air in May. Two lines which Yün liked very much were:

"They softly touch the spring sorrow in my bosom,
And gently stir the longings in her heart."

On the fifth day of the eighth moon in the following year, my mother was going to see Huch'iu with Yün, when Hsienhan suddenly appeared and said, "I am going to Huch'iu, too. Will you come along with me and see a beautiful sing-song girl?" I told my mother to go ahead and agreed to meet her at Pant'ang near Huch'iu. My friend then dragged me to Lenghsiang's place. I saw that Lenghsiang was already in her middle-age, but she had a girl by the name of Hanyüan, who was a very sweet young maiden, still in her teens. Her eyes looked "like an autumn lake that cooled one by its cold splendour." After talking with her for a while, I learnt that she knew very well how to read and write. There was also a younger sister of hers, by the name of Wenyüan, who was still a mere child.

　　余此时初无痴想，且念一杯之叙，非寒士所能酬，而既入个中，私心忐忑，强为酬答。

　　因私谓闲憨曰："余贫士也，子以尤物玩我乎?"

　　闲憨笑曰："非也。今日有友人邀憨园答我，席主为尊客拉去，我代客转邀客。毋烦他虑也。"余始释然。至半塘，两舟相遇，令憨园过舟叩见吾母。芸、憨相见，欢同旧识，携手登山，备览名胜。芸独爱千顷云高旷，坐赏良久。返至野芳滨，畅饮甚欢，并舟而泊。

　　及解维，芸谓余曰："子陪张君，留憨陪妾可乎?"余诺之。返棹至都亭桥，始过船分袂。归家已三鼓。

I had then no thought of going about with a sing-song girl, fully realizing that, as a poor scholar, I could not afford to take part in the feast in such a place. But since I was there already, I tried to get along as best I could.

"Are you trying to seduce me?" I said to Hsienhan secretly.

"No," he replied, "someone had invited me today to a dinner in Hanyüan's place in return for a previous dinner. It happened that the host himself was invited by an important person, and I am acting in his place. Don't you worry!"

I felt then quite relieved. Arriving at Pant'ang, we met my mother's boat, and I asked Hanyüan to go over to her boat and meet her. When Yün and Han met each other, they instinctively took to each other like old friends, and later they went hand-in-hand all over the famous places on the hill. Yün was especially fond of a place called "A Thousand Acres of Clouds" for its loftiness, and she remained there for a long time, lost in admiration of the scenery. We returned to the Waterside of Rural Fragrance where we tied up the boats and had a jolly drinking party together.

When we started on our way home, Yün said, "Will you please go over to the other boat with your friend, while I share this one with Han?" We did as she suggested, and I did not return to my boat until we had passed the Tut'ing Bridge, where we parted from my friend and Hanyüan. It was midnight by the time we returned home.

芸曰："今日得见美而韵者矣。顷已约憨园，明日过我，当为子
图之。"

余骇曰："此非金屋不能贮，穷措大岂敢生此妄想哉！况我两人
伉俪正笃，何必外求？"

芸笑曰："我自爱之，子姑待之。"

明午憨果至。芸殷勤款接，筵中以猜枚——赢吟输饮——为令，
终席无一罗致语。及憨园归，芸曰："顷又与密约，十八日来此结为
姊妹，子宜备牲牢以待。"笑指臂上翡翠钏曰："若见此钏属于憨，事
必谐矣。顷已吐意，未深结其心也。"余姑听之。

"Now I have found a girl who has both beauty and charm," Yün said to me. "I have already asked Hanyüan to come and see us tomorrow, and I'll arrange it for you." I was taken by surprise.

"You know we are not a wealthy family. We can't afford to keep a girl like that, and we are so happily married. Why do you want to find somebody else?"

"But I love her," said Yün smilingly. "You just leave it to me."

The following afternoon, Hanyüan actually came. Yün was very cordial to her and prepared a feast, and we played the finger-guessing game and drank, but during the whole dinner, not a word was mentioned about securing her for me. When Hanyüan had gone, Yün said, "I have secretly made another appointment with her to come on the eighteenth, when we will pledge ourselves as sisters. You must prepare a sacrificial offering for the occasion"; and pointing to the emerald bracelet on her arm, she continued, "if you see this bracelet appear on Hanyüan's arm, you'll understand that she has consented. I have already hinted at it to her, but we haven't got to know each other as thoroughly as I should like to yet." I had to let her have her own way.

　　十八日大雨，憨竟冒雨至，入室良久，始挽手出，见余有羞色，盖翡翠钏已在憨臂矣。焚香结盟后，拟再续前饮。适憨有石湖之游，即别去。

　　芸欣然告余曰："丽人已得，君何以谢媒耶?"余询其详。

　　芸曰："向之秘言，恐憨意另有所属也。顷探之无他，语之曰：'妹知今日之意否?'憨曰：'蒙夫人抬举，真蓬蒿倚玉树也。但吾母望我奢，恐难自主耳，愿彼此缓图之。'脱钏上臂时，又语之曰：'玉取其坚，且有团圆不断之意，妹试笼之，以为先兆。'憨曰：'聚合之权，总在夫人也。'即此观之，憨心已得，所难必者冷香耳，当再图之。"

　　余笑曰："卿将效笠翁之《怜香伴》耶?"

　　芸曰："然。"

　　自此无日不谈憨园矣。后憨为有力者夺去，不果。芸竟以之死。

On the eighteenth, Hanyüan turned up in spite of a pouring rain. She disappeared in the bedroom for a long time before she came out hand-in-hand with Yün. When she saw me, she felt a little shy, for the bracelet was already on her arm. After they had burnt incense and pledged an oath, Yün wanted to have another drink together with her that day. But it happened that Hanyüan had an engagement to go and visit the Shih-hu Lake, and soon she left.

Yün came to me all smiles and said, "Now that I have found a beauty for you, how are you going to reward the go-between?" I asked her for the details.

"I had to broach the topic delicately to her," she said, "because I was afraid that she might have someone else in mind. Now I have learnt that there isn't anyone, and I asked her, 'Do you understand why we have this pledge today?' 'I should feel greatly honoured if I could come to your home, but my mother is expecting a lot of me and I can't decide by myself. We will watch and see,' she replied. As I was putting on the bracelet, I told her again, 'The jade is chosen for its hardness as a token of fidelity and the bracelet's roundness is a symbol of everlasting faithfulness. Meanwhile, please put it on as a token of our pledge. She replied that everything depends on me. So it seems that she is willing herself. The only difficulty is her mother, Lenghsiang. We will wait and see how it turns out."

"Are you going to enact the comedy *Lianhsiangpan* of Li Liweng right in our home?"

"Yes!" Yün replied.

From that time on, not a day passed without her mentioning Hanyüan's name. Eventually Hanyüan was married by force to some influential person, and our arrangements did not come off. And Yün actually died of grief on this account.

Chapter Two

THE LITTLE
PLEASURES OF LIFE

卷二·闲情记趣

　　余忆童稚时，能张目对日，明察秋毫。见藐小微物，必细察其纹理，故时有物外之趣。夏蚊成雷，私拟作群鹤舞空。心之所向，则或千或百，果然鹤也。昂首观之，项为之强。又留蚊于素帐中，徐喷以烟，使其冲烟飞鸣，作青云白鹤观，果如鹤唳云端，怡然称快。于土墙凹凸处，花台小草丛杂处，常蹲其身，使与台齐，定神细视，以丛草为林，以虫蚁为兽，以土砾凸者为丘，凹者为壑，神游其中，怡然自得。

I remember that when I was a child, I could stare at the sun with wide, open eyes. I could see the tiniest objects, and loved to observe the fine grains and patterns of small things, from which I derived a romantic, unworldly pleasure. When mosquitoes were humming round in summer, I transformed them in my imagination into a company of storks dancing in the air. And when I regarded them that way, they were real storks to me, flying by the hundreds and thousands, and I would look up at them until my neck was stiff. Again, I kept a few mosquitoes inside a white curtain and blew a puff of smoke round them, so that to me they became a company of white storks flying among the blue clouds, and their humming was to me the song of storks singing in high heaven, which delighted me intensely. Sometimes I would squat by a broken, earthen wall, or by a little bush on a raised flower-bed, with my eyes on the same level as the flower-bed itself, and there I would look and look, transforming in my mind the little plot of grass into a forest and the ants and insects into wild animals. The little elevations on the ground became my hills, and the depressed areas became my valleys, and my spirit wandered in that world at leisure.

　　一日，见二虫斗草间，观之正浓，忽有庞然大物拔山倒树而来，盖一癞虾蟆也，舌一吐而二虫尽为所吞。余年幼方出神，不觉呀然惊恐。神定，捉虾蟆，鞭数十，驱之别院。年长思之，二虫之斗，盖图奸不从也。古语云："奸近杀"，虫亦然耶？贪此生涯，卵为蚯蚓所哈（吴俗呼阳曰卵），肿不能便。捉鸭开口哈之，婢妪偶释手，鸭颠其颈作吞噬状，惊而大哭；传为话柄。此皆幼时闲情也。

One day, I saw two little insects fighting among the grass, and while I was all absorbed watching the fight, there suddenly appeared a big monster, overturning my hills and tearing up my forest—it was a little toad. With one lick of his tongue, he swallowed up the two little insects. I was so lost in my young imaginary world that I was taken unawares and quite frightened. When I had recovered myself, I caught the toad, struck it several dozen times and chased it out of the courtyard. Thinking of this incident afterwards when I was grown up, I understood that these two little insects were committing adultery by rape. "The wages of sin is death." so says an ancient proverb, and I wondered whether it was true of the insects also. I was a naughty boy, and once my ball (for we call the genital organ a "ball" in Soochow) was bitten by an earthworm and became swollen. [Believing that the duck's saliva would act as an antidote for insect bites,] they held a duck over it, but the maid-servant, who was holding the duck, accidentally let her hand go, and the duck was going to swallow it. I got frightened and screamed. People used to tell this story to make fun of me. These were the little incidents of my childhood days.

　　及长，爱花成癖，喜剪盆树。识张兰坡，始精剪枝养节之法，继悟接花叠石之法。花以兰为最，取其幽香韵致也，而瓣品之稍堪入谱者不可多得。兰坡临终时，赠余荷瓣素心春兰一盆，皆肩平心阔，茎细瓣净，可以入谱者。余珍如拱璧。值余幕游于外，芸能亲为灌溉，花叶颇茂。不二年，一旦忽萎死。起根视之，皆白如玉，且兰芽勃然。初不可解，以为无福消受，浩叹而已。事后始悉有人欲分不允，故用滚汤灌杀也。从此誓不植兰。

　　次取杜鹃，虽无香而色可久玩，且易剪裁。以芸惜枝怜叶，不忍畅剪，故难成树。其他盆玩皆然。

When I was grown up, I loved flowers very much and was very fond of training pot flowers and pot plants. When I knew Chang Lanp'o, I learnt from him the secrets of trimming branches and protecting joints, and later the art of grafting trees and making rockeries. The orchid was prized most among all the flowers because of its subdued fragrance and graceful charm, but it was difficult to obtain really good classic varieties. At the end of his days, Lanp'o presented me with a pot of orchids, whose flowers had lotus-shaped petals; the centre of the flowers was broad and white, the petals were very neat and even at the "shoulders," and the stems were very slender. This type was classical, and I prized it like a piece of old jade. When I was working away from home, Yün used to take care of it personally and it grew beautifully. After two years, it died suddenly one day. I dug up its roots and found that they were white like marble, while nothing was wrong with the sprouts, either. At first, I could not understand this, but ascribed it with a sigh merely to my own bad luck, which might be unworthy to keep such flowers. Later on, I found out that someone had asked for some off-shoots from the same pot, had been refused, and had therefore killed it by pouring boiling water over it. Thenceforth I swore I would never grow orchids again.

Next in preference came the azalea. Although it had no smell, its flowers lasted a longer time and were very beautiful to look at, in addition to its being easy to train up. Yün loved these flowers so much that she would not stand for too much cutting and trimming, and, consequently, it was difficult to make them grow in proper form. The same thing was true of the other flowers.

　　惟每年篱东菊绽，秋兴成癖。喜摘插瓶，不爱盆玩。非盆玩不足观，以家无园圃，不能自植，贷于市者，俱丛杂无致，故不取耳。其插花朵，数宜单，不宜双。每瓶取一种，不取二色。瓶口取阔大，不取窄小，阔大者舒展不拘。自五七花至三四十花，必于瓶口中一丛怒起，以不散漫，不挤轧，不靠瓶口为妙；所谓"起把宜紧"也。或亭亭玉立，或飞舞横斜。花取参差，间以花蕊，以免飞钹耍盘之病。叶取不乱，梗取不强。用针宜藏，针长宁断之，毋令针针露梗，所谓"瓶口宜清"也。视桌之大小，一桌三瓶至七瓶而止，多则眉目不分，即同市井之菊屏矣。几之高低，自三四寸至二尺五六寸而止；必须参差高下，互相照应，以气势联络为上。若中高两低，后高前低，成排对列，又犯俗所谓"锦灰堆"矣。或密或疏，或进或出，全在会心者得画意乃可。

The chrysanthemum, however, was my passion in the autumn of every year. I loved to arrange these flowers in vases instead of raising them in pots, not because I did not want to have them that way, but because I had no garden in my home and could not take care of them myself. What I bought at the market were not properly trained and not to my liking. When arranging chrysanthemum flowers in vases, one should take an odd, not an even, number and each vase should have flowers of only one colour. The mouth of the vase should be broad, so that the flowers could lie easily together. Whether there be half a dozen flowers or even thirty or forty of them in a vase, they should be so arranged as to come up together straight from the mouth of the vase, neither overcrowded, nor too much spread out, nor leaning against the mouth of the vase. This is called "keeping the handle firm." Sometimes they can stand gracefully erect, and sometimes spread out in different directions. In order to avoid a bare monotonous effect, they should be mixed with some flower buds and arranged in a kind of studied disorderliness. The leaves should not be too thick and the stems should not be too stiff. In using pins to hold the stems up, one should break the long pins off, rather than expose them. This is called "keeping the mouth of the vase clear." Place from three to seven vases on a table, depending on the size of the latter, for if there were too many of them, they would be overcrowded, looking like chrysanthemum screens at the market. The stands for the vases should be of different height, from three or four inches to two and a half feet, so that the different vases at different heights would balance one another and belong intimately to one another as in a picture with unity of composition. To put one vase high in the centre with two low at the sides, or to put a low one in front and a tall one behind, or to arrange them in symmetrical pairs, would be to create what is vulgarly called "a heap of gorgeous refuse." Proper spacing and arrangement must depend on the individual who has an understanding of pictorial composition.

　　若盆碗盘洗，用漂青，松香，榆皮，面和油，先熬以稻灰，收成胶。以铜片按钉向上，将膏火化，粘铜片于盘碗盆洗中。俟冷，将花用铁丝扎把，插于钉上，宜斜偏取势，不可居中，更宜枝疏叶清，不可拥挤；然后加水，用碗沙少许掩铜片，使观者疑丛花生于碗底方妙。

　　若以木本花果插瓶，剪裁之法（不能色色自觅，倩人攀折者每不合意），必先执在手中，横斜以观其势，反侧以取其态。相定之后，剪去杂枝，以疏瘦古怪为佳。再思其梗如何入瓶，或折或曲，插入瓶口，方免背叶侧花之患。

In the case of flower bowls or open dishes, the method of making a support
for the flowers is to mix pitch and refined resin with elm bark, flour and oil,
and heat up the mixture with hot hay ashes until it becomes a kind of glue, and
with it glue some nails upside down on to a piece of copper. This copper plate
can then be heated up and glued on to the bottom of the bowl or dish. When
it is cold, tie the flowers in groups by means of wire and stick them on those
nails. The flowers should be allowed to incline sideways and not shoot up from
the centre; it is also important that the stems and leaves should not come too
closely together. After this is done, put some water in the bowl and cover up
the copper support with some clean sand, so that the flowers will seem to grow
directly from the bottom of the bowl.

When picking branches from flower-trees for decoration in vases, it is
important to know how to trim them before putting them in the vase, for
one cannot always go and pick them oneself, and those picked by others are
often unsatisfactory. Hold the branch in your hand and turn it back and forth
in different ways in order to see how it lies most expressively. After one has
made up one's mind about it, lop off the superfluous branches, with the idea of
making the twig look thin and sparse and quaintly beautiful. Next think how
the stem is going to lie in the vase and with what kind of bend, so that when it
is put there, the leaves and flowers can be shown to the best advantage.

　　若一枝到手，先拘定其梗之直者插瓶中，势必枝乱梗强，花侧叶背，既难取态，更无韵致矣。折梗打曲之法：锯其梗之半而嵌以砖石，则直者曲矣。如患梗倒，敲一二钉以管之。即枫叶竹枝，乱草荆棘，均堪入选。或绿竹一竿，配以枸杞数粒，几茎细草，伴以荆棘两枝，苟位置得宜，另有世外之趣。

　　若新栽花木，不妨歪斜取势，听其叶侧，一年后枝叶自能向上。如树树直栽，即难取势矣。

If one just takes any old branch in hand, chooses a straight section and puts it in the vase, the consequence will be that the stem will be too stiff, the branches will be too close together and the flowers and leaves will be turned in the wrong direction, devoid of all charm and expression. To make a straight twig crooked, cut a mark half-way across the stem and insert a little piece of broken brick or stone at the joint; the straight branch will then become a bent one. In case the stem is too weak, put one or two pins to strengthen it. By means of this method, even maple leaves and bamboo twigs or even ordinary grass and thistles will look very well for decoration. Put a twig of green bamboo side by side with a few berries of Chinese matrimony vine or arrange some fine blades of grass together with some branches of thistle. They will look quite poetic, if the arrangement is correct.

In planting new trees, it does not matter if the trunk comes up from the ground at an angle, for if let alone for a year, it will grow upwards by itself. On the other hand, if one lets the stem come up in a perpendicular line, it will be difficult later on for it to have a dynamic posture.

　　至剪裁盆树，先取根露鸡爪者，左右剪成三节，然后起枝。一枝
一节，七枝到顶，或九枝到顶。枝忌对节如肩臂，节忌臃肿如鹤膝。
须盘旋出枝，不可光留左右，以避赤胸露背之病。又不可前后直出。
有名"双起"、"三起"者，一根而起两三树也。如根无爪形，便成插树，
故不取。

　　然一树剪成，至少得三四十年。余生平仅见吾乡万翁名彩章者，
一生剪成数树。又在扬州商家见有虞山游客携送黄杨翠柏各一盆，惜
乎明珠暗投。余未见其可也。若留枝盘如宝塔，扎枝曲如蚯蚓者，便
成匠气矣。

As to the training of pot plants, one should choose those with claw-like roots coming above the surface of the ground. Lop off the first three branches from the ground before allowing the next one to grow up, making a bend at every point where a new branch starts off. There should be seven such bends, or perhaps nine, from the lower end of a tree to its top. It is against good taste to have swollen joints at these bends, or to have two branches growing directly opposite each other at the same point. These must branch off in all directions from different points, for if one only allows those on the right and left to grow up, the effect will be very bare, or "the chest and back will be exposed," as we say. Nor, for instance, should they grow straight from the front or behind. There are "double-trunked" and "treble-trunked" trees which all spring from the same root above the ground. If the root were not claw-shaped, they would look like planted sticks and would on that account be disqualified.

The proper training of a tree, however, takes at least thirty to forty years. In my whole life, I have seen only one person, old Wan Ts'aichang of my district, who succeeded in training several trees in his life. Once I also saw at the home of a merchant at Yangchow two pots, one of boxwood and one of cypress, presented to him by a friend from Yüshan, but this was like casting pearls before swine. Outside these cases, I have not seen any really good ones. Trees whose branches are trained in different horizontal circles going up like a pagoda or whose branches turn round and round like earthworms are incurably vulgar.

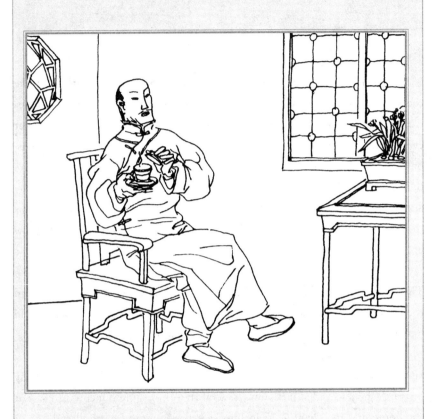

　　点缀盆中花石，小景可以入画，大景可以入神。一瓯清茗，神能趋入其中，方可供幽斋之玩。种水仙无灵璧石，余尝以炭之有石意者代之。黄芽菜心，其白如玉，取大小五七枝，用沙土植长方盆内，以炭代石，黑白分明，颇有意思。以此类推，幽趣无穷，难以枚举。如石菖蒲结子，用冷米汤同嚼喷炭上，置阴湿地，能长细菖蒲；随意移养盆碗中，茸茸可爱。以老莲子磨薄两头，入蛋壳使鸡翼之，俟雏成取出。用久年燕巢泥加天门冬十分之二，捣烂拌匀，植于小器中，灌以河水，晒以朝阳；花发大如酒杯，叶缩如碗口，亭亭可爱。

When arranging miniature sceneries with flowers and stones in a pot, design so that a small one could suggest a painting, and a big one the infinite. One should make it so that, with a pot of tea, one could lose oneself in a world of imagination; and only this kind should be kept in one's private studio for enjoyment. Once I planted some narcissus and could not find any pebbles from Lingpi for use in the pot, and I substituted them with pieces of coal that looked like rocks. One can also take five or seven pieces of yellow-brimmed white cabbage of different size, whose core is white like jade, and plant them in sand in an oblong earthen basin, decorated with charcoal instead of pebbles. The black of the charcoal will then contrast vividly with the white of the cabbage, quite interesting to look at. It is impossible to enumerate all the possible variations, but if one exercises one's ingenuity, it will be found to be an endless source of pleasure. For instance, one can take some calamus seeds in the mouth, chew them together with cold rice soup, and blow them on to pieces of charcoal. Keep them in a dark damp place and fine little calamus will grow from them. These pieces of charcoal can then be placed in any flower basin, looking like moss-covered rocks. Or one can take some old lotus seeds, grind off slightly both ends, and put them in an egg-shell, making a hen sit on it together with other eggs. When the little chickens are hatched, take the egg out also and plant the old lotus seeds in old clay from swallows' nests, prepared with twenty per cent of ground asparagus. Keep these then in a small vessel filled with river water, and expose them to the morning sun. When the flowers bloom, they will be only the size of a wine cup, while the leaves will be about the size of a bowl, very cute and beautiful to look at.

　　若夫园亭楼阁，套室回廊，叠石成山，栽花取势，又在大中见小，小中见大，虚中有实，实中有虚，或藏或露，或浅或深，不仅在"周、迴、曲、折"四字，又不在地广石多，徒烦工费。或掘地堆土成山，间以块石，杂以花草，篱用梅编，墙以藤引，则无山而成山矣。大中见小者：散漫处植易长之竹，编易茂之梅以屏之。小中见大者：窄院之墙，宜凹凸其形，饰以绿色，引以藤蔓，嵌大石，凿字作碑记形。推窗如临石壁，便觉峻峭无穷。虚中有实者：或山穷水尽处，一折而豁然开朗；或轩阁设厨处，一开而可通别院。实中有虚者：开门于不通之院，映以竹石，如有实无也；设矮栏于墙头，如上有月台，而实虚也。

As to the planning of garden pavilions, towers, winding corridors and out-houses, the designing of rockery and the training of flower-trees, one should try to show the small in the big, and the big in the small, and provide for the real in the unreal and for the unreal in the real. One reveals and conceals alternately, making it sometimes apparent and sometimes hidden. This is not just rhythmic irregularity, nor does it depend on having a wide space and great expenditure of labour and material. Pile up a mound with earth dug from the ground and decorate it with rocks, mingled with flowers; use live plum-branches for your fence, and plant creepers over the walls. Thus one can create the effect of a hill out of a flat piece of ground. In the big, open spaces, plant bamboos that grow quickly and train plum-trees with thick branches to screen them off. This is to show the small in the big. When a courtyard is small, the wall should run in a series of convex and concave lines, decorated with green, covered with ivy and inlaid with big slabs of stone with inscriptions on them. Thus when you open your window, you seem to face a rocky hillside, alive with rugged beauty. This is to show the big in the small. Contrive so that an apparently blind alley leads suddenly into an open space and a closet-like door forms the entrance into an unexpected courtyard. This is to provide for the real in the unreal. Let a door lead into a blind courtyard and conceal the view by placing a few bamboo trees and a few rocks before it. Thus you suggest something which is not there. Place low balustrades along the top of a wall so as to suggest a roof garden. This is to provide for the unreal in the real.

贫士屋少人多，当仿吾乡太平船后梢之位置，再加转移。其间台级为床，前后借凑，可作三榻，间以板而裱以纸，则前后上下皆越绝。譬之如行长路，即不觉其窄矣。余夫妇乔寓扬州时，曾仿此法。屋仅两椽，上下卧房、厨灶、客座皆越绝而绰然有余。芸曾笑曰："位置虽精，终非富贵家气象也。"是诚然欤？

余扫墓山中，检有峦纹可观之石。归与芸商曰："用油灰叠宣州石于白石盆，取色匀也。本山黄石虽古朴，亦用油灰，则黄白相间，凿痕毕露，将奈何？"芸曰："择石之顽劣者，捣末于灰痕处，乘湿糁之，干或色同也。"

Poor scholars who live in crowded houses should follow the method of the boatmen in our native district who make clever arrangements with their limited space on the sterns of their boats by devising certain modifications, such as making a series of successive elevations one after another, and using them as beds, of which there may be three in a little room, and separating them with papered wooden partitions. The effect will be compact and wonderful to look at, like surveying a long stretch of road, and one will not feel the cramping of space. When my wife and I were staying at Yangchow, we lived in a house of only two beams, but the two bedrooms, the kitchen and the parlour were all arranged in this method, with an exquisite effect and great saving of space. Yün once said to me laughingly, "The arrangements are exquisite enough, but after all, they lack the luxurious atmosphere of a rich man's house." It was so indeed.

Once I visited my ancestral tombs on the hill and found some pebbles of great beauty, with faint tracings on them. On coming back, I talked it over with Yün, and said, "People mix putty with Hsüanchow stones in white stone basins, because the colours of the two elements blend. These yellow pebbles of this hill, however, are different, and although they are rugged and simple, they will not blend in colour with putty. What can we do?" "Take some of the worse quality," she said, "pound them into small pieces and mix them in the putty before it is dry, and perhaps when it is dry, the colour will be uniform."

　　乃如其言，用宜兴窑长方盆叠起一峰，偏于左而凸于右，背作横方纹，如云林石法；嵬岩凹凸，若临江石矶状。虚一角，用河泥种千瓣白萍。石上植茑萝，俗呼云松。经营数日乃成。至深秋，茑萝蔓延满山，如藤萝之悬石壁，花开正红色。白萍亦透水大放，红白相间。神游其中，如登蓬岛。置之檐下与芸品题：此处宜设水阁，此处宜立茅亭，此处宜凿六字曰"落花流水之间"；此可以居，此可以钓，此可以眺；胸中丘壑，若将移居者然。一夕，猫奴争食，自檐而堕，连盆与架，顷刻碎之。余叹曰："即此小经营，尚干造物忌耶！"两人不禁泪落。

So we did as she suggested, and took a rectangular Yi-hsing earthen basin, on which we piled up a mountain peak on the left coming down in undulations to the right. On its back, we made rugged square lines in the style of rock paintings of Ni Yünlin, so that the whole looked like a rocky precipice overhanging a river. At one corner we made a hollow place, which we filled with mud and planted with multi-leaf white duckweed, while the rocks were planted with dodder. This took us quite a few days to finish. In late autumn, the dodder grew all over the hill, like wistarias hanging down from a rock. The red dodder flowers made a striking contrast to the white duckweed, which had grown luxuriantly, too, from the pond underneath. Looking at it, one could imagine oneself transported to some fairy region. We put this under the eaves, and discussed between ourselves where we should build a covered terrace by the water, where we should put a garden arbour, and where we should put a stone inscription: "Where petals drop and waters flow." And Yün further discussed with me where we could build our home, where we could fish, and where we could go up for a better view of the distance, all so absorbed in it as if we were moving to live in that little imaginary universe. One night, two cats were fighting for food and fell down over the eaves and accidentally broke the whole thing into pieces, basin and all. I sighed and said, "The gods seem to be jealous of even such a little effort of ours." And we both shed tears.

　　静室焚香，闲中雅趣。芸尝以沉速等香，于饭镬蒸透，在炉上设
一铜丝架，离火半寸许，徐徐烘之；其香幽韵而无烟。佛手忌醉鼻嗅，
嗅则易烂。木瓜忌出汗，汗出，用水洗之。惟香橼无忌。佛手、木瓜
亦有供法，不能笔宣。每有人将供妥者随手取嗅，随手置之，即不知
供法者也。

　　余闲居，案头瓶花不绝。芸曰："子之插花，能备风晴雨露，可
谓精妙入神；而画中有草虫一法，盍仿而效之？"

　　余曰："虫踯躅不受制，焉能仿效？"

To burn incense in a quiet room is one of the cultivated pleasures of a leisurely life. Yün used to burn aloes-wood and *shuhsiang* [a kind of fragrant wood from Cambodia]. She used to steam the wood first in a cauldron thoroughly, and then place it on a copper wire net over a stove, about half an inch from the fire. Under the action of the slow fire, the wood would give out a kind of subtle fragrance without any visible smoke. Another thing, the "buddha's fingers" [a variety of citron] should not be smelt by a drunken man, or it would easily rot. It is also bad for the quince to perspire [as under atmospheric changes], and when it does so, one should wash it with water. The citron alone is easy to take care of, because it is not afraid of handling. There are different ways of taking care of the "buddha's fingers" and the quince which cannot be expressed in so many words. I have seen people who take one of these things, which have been properly kept, and handle or smell it in any old way and put it down again roughly, which shows that they do not know the art of preserving these things.

In my home I always had a vase of flowers on my desk. "You know very well about arranging flowers in vases for all kinds of weather," said Yün to me one day. "I think you have really understood the art, but there is a type of painting commonly called 'insects on grass blades,' which you haven't applied yet. Why don't you try?"

"I'm afraid," I replied, "that I cannot hold the insect's legs still. What can I do?"

芸曰："有一法，恐作俑罪过耳。"

余曰："试言之。"

芸曰："虫死色不变。觅螳螂、蝉、蝶之属，以针刺死，用细丝扣虫项系花草间，整其足，或抱梗，或踏叶，宛然如生。不亦善乎?"

余喜，如其法行之，见者无不称绝。求之闺中，今恐未必有此会心者矣。

余与芸寄居锡山华氏，时华夫人以两女从芸识字。乡居院旷，夏日逼人。芸教其家作活花屏法，甚妙。每屏一扇，用木梢二枝，约长四五寸，作矮条凳式，虚其中，横四挡，宽一尺许，四角凿圆眼，插竹编方眼。屏约高六七尺，用砂盆种扁豆，置屏中，盘延屏上，两人可移动。

"I know a way, except that I am afraid it would be too cruel," said Yün.

"Tell me about it," I asked.

"You know that an insect does not change its colour after death. You can find a mantis or cicada or a butterfly; kill it with a pin and use a fine wire to tie its neck to the flowers, arranging its legs so that they either hold on to the stem or rest on the leaves. It would then look like a live one. Don't you think it is very good?"

I was quite delighted and did as she suggested, and many of our friends thought it very wonderful. I am afraid it is difficult to find ladies nowadays who show such an understanding of things.

When I was staying with my friend Mr. Hua at Hsishan with Yün, Mrs. Hua used to ask Yün to teach her two daughters reading. In that country house, the yard was wide open and the glare of the summer sun was very oppressive. Yün taught them a method of making movable screens of growing flowers. Every screen consisted of a single piece. She took two little pieces of wood about four or five inches long, and laid them parallel like a low stool, with the hollow top filled by four horizontal bars over a foot long. At the four corners, she made little round holes on which she stuck a trellis-work made of bamboo. The trellis was six or seven feet high and on its bottom was placed a pot of peas which would then grow up and entwine round the bamboo trellis. This could be easily moved by two persons.

多编数屏，随意遮拦，恍如绿阴满窗，透风蔽日，迂回曲折，随时可更，故曰"活花屏"。有此一法，即一切藤本香草，随地可用。此真乡居之良法也。

友人鲁半舫，名璋，字春山，善写松柏或梅菊，工隶书，兼工铁笔。余寄居其家之萧爽楼一年有半。楼共五椽，东向，余居其三。晦明风雨，可以远眺。庭中木犀一株，清香撩人。有廊有厢，地极幽静。移居时，有一仆一妪，并挈其小女来。仆能成衣，妪能纺绩；于是芸绣，妪绩，仆则成衣，以供薪水。

One can make several of these things and place them wherever one pleases, before windows or doors, and they will look like living plants, casting their green shade into the house, warding off the sun and yet allowing the wind to come through. They can be placed in any irregular formation, adjustable according to time and circumstances, and are, therefore, called "movable flower screens." With this method, one can use any kind of fragrant weeds of the creeper family, instead of peas. It is an excellent arrangement for people staying in the country.

My friend Lu Panfang's name was Chang and his literary name Ch'ünshan. He was very good at painting pine-trees and cypresses, plum blossoms and chrysanthemums, as well as writing the *lishu* style of calligraphy, besides specializing in carving seals. I stayed in his home called Hsiaoshuanglou for a year and a half. The house faced east and consisted of five beams, of which I occupied three. From it one could get a beautiful view of the distance in rain or shine. In the middle of the court, there was a tree, the *Osmanthus fragrans*, which filled the air with a kind of delicate fragrance. There were corridors and living rooms, and the place was quite secluded. When I went there, I brought along a man-servant and an old woman, who also brought with them a young daughter. The man-servant could make dresses and the old woman could spin; therefore Yün did embroidery, the old woman spun and the man-servant made dresses to provide for our daily expenses.

　　余素爱客，小酌必行令。芸善不费之烹庖，瓜蔬鱼虾，一经芸手，便有意外味。同人知余贫，每出杖头钱，作竟日叙。余又好洁，地无纤尘，且无拘束，不嫌放纵。

　　时有杨补凡名昌绪，善人物写真；袁少迂名沛，工山水；王星澜名岩，工花卉翎毛；爱萧爽楼幽雅，皆携画具来，余则从之学画。写草篆，镌图章，加以润笔，交芸备茶酒供客，终日品诗论画而已。更有夏淡安、揖山两昆季，并缪山音、知白两昆季，及蒋韵香、陆橘香、周啸霞、郭小愚、华杏帆、张闲憨诸君子，如梁上之燕，自去自来。芸则拔钗沽酒，不动声色，良辰美景，不放轻过。今则天各一方，风流云散，兼之玉碎香埋，不堪回首矣！

I was by nature very fond of guests and whenever we had a little drinking party, I insisted on having wine-games. Yün was very clever at preparing inexpensive dishes; ordinary foodstuffs like melon, vegetables, fish and shrimps had a special flavour when prepared by her. My friends knew that I was poor, and often helped pay the expenses in order that we might get together and talk for the whole day. I was very keen on keeping the place spotlessly clean, and was, besides, fond of free and easy ways with my friends.

At this time, there were a group of friends, like Yang Pufan, also called Ch'anghsü, who specialized in portrait sketches; Yüan Shaoyü, also called P'ai, who specialized in painting landscape; and Wang Hsing-lan, also called Yen, good at painting flowers and birds. They all liked the Hsiaoshuanglou because of its seclusion, so they would bring their painting utensils to the place and I learnt painting from them. They would then either write "grass-script" or "*chüan-script*" or carve seals, from which we made some money which we turned over to Yün to defray expenses for teas and dinners. The whole day long, we were occupied in discussing poetry or painting only. There were, moreover, friends like the brothers Hsia Tan-an and Hsia Yishan, the brothers Miao Shanyin and Miao Chihpo, Chiang Yünhsiang, Loh Chühsiang, Chou Hsiaohsia, Kuo Hsiaoyü, Hua Hsingfan, and Chang Hsienhan. These friends came and went as they pleased, like the swallows by the eaves. Yün would take off her hairpin and sell it for wine without a second's thought, for she would not let a beautiful day pass without company. To-day these friends are scattered to the four corners of the earth like clouds dispersed by a storm, and the woman I loved is dead, like broken jade and buried incense. How sad indeed to look back upon these things!

　　萧爽楼有四忌：谈官宦升迁，公廨时事，入股时文，看牌掷色；有犯必罚酒五斤。有四取：慷慨豪爽，风流蕴藉，落拓不羁，澄静缄默。长夏无事，考对为会。每会八人，每人各携青蚨二百。先拈阄，得第一者为主考，关防别座；第二者为誊录，亦就座；余作举子，各于誊录处取纸一条，盖用印章。主考出五七言各一句，刻香为限，行立构思，不准交头私语。对就后投入一匣，方许就座。各人交卷毕，誊录启匣，并录一册，转呈主考，以杜徇私。

Among the friends at Hsiaoshuanglou, four things were tabooed: firstly, talking about people's official promotions; secondly, gossiping about law-suits and current affairs; thirdly, discussing the conventional eight-legged essays for the imperial examinations; and fourthly, playing cards and dice. Whoever broke any of these rules was penalized to provide five catties of wine. On the other hand, there were four things which we all approved: generosity, romantic charm, free and easy ways, and quietness. In the long summer days when we had nothing to do, we used to hold examinations among ourselves. At those parties, there would be eight persons, each bringing two hundred cash along. We began by drawing lots, and the one who got the first would be the official examiner, seated on top by himself, while the second one would be the official recorder, also seated in his place. The others would then be the candidates, each taking a slip of paper, properly stamped with a seal, from the official recorder. The examiner then gave out a line of seven words and one of five words, with which each of us was to make the best couplet. The time limit was the burning of a joss-stick and we were to tease our brains standing or walking about, but were not allowed to exchange words with each other. When a candidate had made the couplets, he placed them in a special box and then returned to his seat. After all the papers had been handed in, the official recorder then opened the box and copied them together in a book, which he submitted to the examiner, thus safeguarding against any partiality on the latter's part.

　　十六对中取七言三联，五言三联。六联中取第一者即为后任主考，第二者为誊录。每人有两联不取者罚钱二十文，取一联者免罚十文，过限者倍罚。一场，主考得钱百文。一日可十场，积钱千文，酒资大畅矣。惟芸议为官卷，准坐而构思。

　　杨补凡为余夫妇写载花小影，神情确肖。是夜月色颇佳，兰影上粉墙，别有幽致。星澜醉后兴发曰："补凡能为君写真，我能为花图影。"

　　余笑曰："花影能如人影否？"

　　星澜取素纸铺于墙，即就兰影用墨浓淡图之。日间取视，虽不成画，而花叶萧疏，自有月下之趣。芸甚宝之，各有题咏。

Of these couplets submitted, three of the seven-word lines and three of the five-word lines were to be chosen as the best. The one who turned in the best of these six chosen couplets would then be the official examiner for the next round, and the second best would be the official recorder. One who had two couplets failing to be chosen would be fined twenty cash, one failing in one couplet fined ten cash, and failures handed in beyond the time limit would be fined twice the amount. The official examiner would get one hundred cash "incense money." Thus we could have ten examinations in a day and provide a thousand cash with which to buy wine and have a grand drinking party. Yün's paper alone was considered special and exempt from fine, and she was allowed the privilege of thinking out her lines on her seat.

One day Yang Pufan made a sketch of Yün and myself working at a garden with wonderful likeness. On that night, the moon was very bright and was casting a wonderfully picturesque shadow of an orchid flower on the white wall. Inspired by some hard drinking, Hsing-lan said to me, "Pufan can paint your portrait sketch, but I can paint the shadows of flowers."

"Will the sketch of flowers be as good as that of a man?" I asked.

Then Hsing-lan took a piece of paper and placed it against the wall, on which he traced the shadow of the orchid flower with dark and light inkings. When we looked at it in the day-time, there was a kind of haziness about the lines of leaves and flowers, suggestive of the moonlight, although it could not be called a real painting. Yün liked it very much and all my friends wrote their inscriptions on it.

　　苏城有南园、北园二处，菜花黄时，苦无酒家小饮；携盒而往，对花冷饮，殊无意味。或议就近觅饮者，或议看花归饮者，终不如对花热饮为快。众议未定。芸笑曰："明日但各出杖头钱，我自担炉火来。"众笑曰："诺。"众去，余问曰："卿果自往乎?"芸曰："非也。妾见市中卖馄饨者，其担锅、灶无不备，盍雇之而往? 妾先烹调端整，到彼处再一下锅，茶酒两便。"

　　余曰："酒菜固便矣。茶乏烹具。"

　　芸曰："携一砂罐去，以铁叉串罐柄，去其锅，悬于行灶中，加柴火煎茶，不亦便乎?"

There are two places in Soochow called the South Garden and the North Garden. We would go there when the rape flowers were in bloom, but there was no wine shop nearby where we could have a drink. If we brought eatables along in a basket, there was little fun drinking cold wine in the company of the flowers. Some proposed that we should look for some place to get a drink in the neighbourhood, and others suggested that we should look at the flowers first and then come back for a drink, but this was never quite the ideal thing, which should be to drink warm wine in the presence of flowers. While no one could make any satisfactory suggestion, Yün smiled and said, "Tomorrow you people provide the money and I'll carry a stove to the place myself." "Very well," they all said. When my friends had left, I asked Yün how she was going to do it. "I am not going to carry it myself," she said. "I have seen *wonton* sellers in the streets who carry along a stove and a pan and everything we need. We could just ask one of these fellows to go along with us. I'll prepare the dishes first, and when we arrive, all we need is just to heat them up, and we will have everything ready including tea and wine."

"Well, but what about the kettle for boiling tea?"

"We could carry along an earthen pot," she said, "remove the *wonton* seller's pan and suspend the pot over the fire by a spike. This will then serve us as a kettle for boiling tea, won't it?"

　　余鼓掌称善。街头有鲍姓者，卖馄饨为业，以百钱雇其担，约以明日午后。鲍欣然允议。明日看花者至，余告以故，众咸叹服。饭后同往，并带席垫，至南园，择柳阴下团坐。先烹茗，饮毕，然后暖酒烹肴。是时风和日丽，遍地黄金，青衫红袖，越阡度陌，蝶蜂乱飞，令人不饮自醉。既而酒肴俱熟，坐地大嚼。担者颇不俗，拉与同饮。游人见之，莫不羡为奇想。杯盘狼藉，各已陶然，或坐或卧，或歌或啸。红日将颓，余思粥，担者即为买米煮之，果腹而归。

I clapped my hands in applause. There was a *wonton* seller by the name of Pao, whom we asked to go along with us the following afternoon, offering to pay him a hundred cash, to which Pao readily consented. The following day my friends, who were going to see the flowers, arrived. I told them about the arrangements, and they were all amazed at Yün's ingenious idea. We started off after lunch, bringing along with us some straw mats and cushions. When we had arrived at the South Garden, we chose a place under the shade of willow trees, and sat together in a circle on the ground. First we boiled some tea, and after drinking it, we warmed up the wine and heated up the dishes. The sun was beautiful and the breeze was gentle, while the yellow rape flowers in the field looked like a stretch of gold, with gaily dressed young men and women passing by the rice fields and bees and butterflies flitting to and fro—a sight which could make one drunk without any liquor. Very soon the wine and dishes were ready and we sat together on the ground drinking and eating. The *wonton* seller was quite a likeable person and we asked him to join us. People who saw us thus enjoying ourselves thought it quite a novel idea. Then the cups, bowls and dishes lay about in great disorder on the ground, while we were already slightly drunk, some sitting and some lying down, and some singing or yelling. When the sun was going down, I wanted to eat congee, and the *wonton* seller bought some rice and cooked it for us. We then came back with a full belly.

芸问曰："今日之游乐乎？"

众曰："非夫人之力不及此。"大笑而散。

贫士起居服食，以及器皿房舍，宜省俭而雅洁。省俭之法，曰"就事论事"。余爱小饮，不喜多菜。芸为置一梅花盒，用二寸白磁深碟六只，中置一只，外置五只，用灰漆就，其形如梅花。底盖均起凹楞，盖之上有柄如花蒂，置之案头，如一朵墨梅覆桌；启盖视之，如菜装于花瓣中。一盒六色，二三知己可以随意取食。食完再添。另做矮边圆盘一只，以便放杯、箸、酒壶之类，随处可摆，移掇亦便。即食物省俭之一端也。

"Did you enjoy it today?" asked Yün.

"We would not have enjoyed it so much, had it not been for Madame!" all of us exclaimed. Then merrily we parted.

A poor scholar should try to be economical in the matter of food, clothing, house and furniture, but at the same time be clean and artistic. In order to be economical, one should "manage according to the needs of the occasion," as the saying goes. I was very fond of having nice little suppers with a little liquor, but did not care for many dishes. Yün used to make a tray with a plum-blossom design. It consisted of six deep dishes of white porcelain, two inches in diameter, one in the centre and the other five grouped round it, painted grey and looking like a plum flower. Both its bottom and its top were bevelled and there was a handle on the top resembling the stem of a plum flower, so that, when placed on the table, it looked like a regular plum blossom dropped on the table, and on opening, the different vegetables were found to be contained in the petals of the flower. A case like this with six different dishes would be quite enough to serve a dinner for two or three close friends. If second helping was needed, more could be added. Besides this, we made another round tray with a low border for holding chopsticks, cups and the wine pot. These were easily moved about and one could have the dinner served at any place one wished. This is an example of economy in the matter of food.

　　余之小帽领袜，皆芸自做。衣之破者移东补西，必整必洁；色取
暗淡，以免垢迹，既可出客，又可家常。此又服饰省俭之一端也。初
至萧爽楼中，嫌其暗，以白纸糊壁，遂亮。夏月楼下去窗，无栏干，
觉空洞无遮拦。芸曰："有旧竹帘在，何不以帘代栏？"

　　余曰："如何？"

　　芸曰："用竹数根，黝黑色，一竖一横，留出走路。截半帘，搭
在横竹上，垂至地，高与桌齐。中竖短竹四根，用麻线扎定，然后于
横竹搭帘处，寻旧黑布条，连横竹里缝之。既可遮拦饰观，又不费钱。"
此"就事论事"之一法也。以此推之，古人所谓"竹头木屑皆有用"，
良有以也。

Yün also made me my collars, socks and my little cap. When my clothes were torn, she would cut out one piece to mend another, making it always look very neat and tidy. I used to choose quiet colours for my clothes, for the reason that dirty spots would not show easily, and one could wear them both at home and abroad. This is an instance of economy in the matter of dress. When I first took up my residence at the Hsiaoshuanglou, I found the rooms too dark, but after papering the walls with white paper, they were quite bright again. During the summer months, the ground floor was quite open, because the windows had all been taken down, and we felt that the place lacked privacy. "There is an old bamboo screen," suggested Yün, "why don't we use it and let it serve in place of a railing?"

"But how?" I asked.

"Take a few pieces of bamboo of black colour," she replied, "and make them into a square, leaving room for people to pass out and in. Cut off half of the bomboo screen and fasten it on the horizontal bamboo, about the height of a table, letting the screen come down to the ground. Then put four vertical pieces of short bamboo in the centre, fasten these in place by means of a string, and then find some old strips of black cloth and wrap them up together with the horizontal bar with needle and thread. It would give a little privacy and would look quite well, besides being inexpensive." This is an instance of "managing according to the needs of the occasion." This goes to prove the truth of the ancient saying that "slips of bamboo and chips of wood all have their uses."

夏月荷花初开时，晚含而晓放。芸用小纱囊撮茶叶少许，置花心。明早取出，烹天泉水泡之，香韵尤绝。

When the lotus flowers bloom in summer, they close at night and open in the morning. Yün used to put some tea leaves in a little silk bag and place it in the centre of the flower at night. We would take it out the next morning, and make tea with spring water, which would then have a very delicate flavour.

Chapter Three

SORROW

卷三·坎坷记愁

　　人生坎坷何为乎来哉？往往皆自作孽耳。余则非也！多情重诺，爽直不羁，转因之为累。况吾父稼夫公慷慨豪侠，急人之难，成人之事，嫁人之女，抚人之儿，指不胜屈；挥金如土，多为他人。余夫妇居家，偶有需用，不免典质；始则移东补西，继则左支右绌。谚云："处家人情，非钱不行。"先起小人之议，渐招同室之讥。"女子无才便是德"，真千古至言也！

　　余虽居长而行三，故上下呼芸为"三娘"；后忽呼为"三太太"。始而戏呼，继成习惯，甚至尊卑长幼皆以"三太太"呼之。此家庭之变机欤？

Why is it that there are sorrows and hardships in this life? Usually they are due to one's own fault, but this was not the case with me. I was fond of friendship, proud of keeping my word, and by nature frank and straightforward, for which I eventually suffered. My father Chiafu, too, was a very generous man; he used to help people in trouble, bring up other people's sons and marry off other people's daughters in innumerable instances, spending money like dirt, all for the sake of other people. My wife and I often had to pawn things when we were in need of money, and while at first we managed to make both ends meet, gradually our purse became thinner and thinner. As the proverb says, "To run a family and mix socially, money is the first essential." At first we incurred the criticism of the busybodies, and then even people of our own family began to make sarcastic remarks. Indeed "absence of talent in a woman is synonymous with virtue," as the ancient proverb says.

I was born the third son of my family, although the eldest; hence they used to call Yün "*san niang*" at home, but this was later suddenly changed into "*san t'ait'ai*." This began at first in fun, later became a general practice, and even relatives of all ranks, high and low, addressed her as "*san t'ait'ai*."[1] I wonder if this was a sign of the beginning of family dissension.

[1] "*San*" means "number three." The meaning of "*niang*" and "*t'ait'ai*" varies with local usage, but generally "*niang*" refers to a young married woman in a big household, while "*t'ait'ai*" suggests the mistress of an independent home. — *Tr.*

　　乾隆乙巳，随侍吾父于海宁官舍。芸于吾家书中附寄小函。吾父曰：
"媳妇既能笔墨，汝母家信付彼司之。"后家庭偶有闲言，吾母疑其述
事不当，乃不令代笔。吾父见信非芸手笔，询余曰："汝妇病耶？"余
即作札问之，亦不答。久之，吾父怒曰："想汝妇不屑代笔耳！"迨余
归，探知委曲，欲为婉剖。芸急止之曰："宁受责于翁，勿失欢于姑也。"
竟不自白。

　　庚戌之春，予又随侍吾父于邗江幕中。有同事俞孚亭者，挈眷居焉。
吾父谓孚亭曰："一生辛苦，常在客中，欲觅一起居服役之人而不可得。
儿辈果能仰体亲意，当于家乡觅一人来，庶语音相合。"

When I was staying with my father at the Haining yamen in 1785, Yün used to enclose personal letters of hers along with the regular family correspondence. Seeing this, my father said that, since Yün could write letters, she should be entrusted with the duty of writing letters for my mother. It happened that there was a little family gossip and my mother suspected that it had leaked out through Yün's letters, and stopped her writing. When my father saw that it was not Yün's handwriting, he asked me, "Is your wife sick?" I then wrote to enquire from her, but got no reply. After some time had elapsed, my father was angry with her and spoke to me, "Your wife seems to think it beneath her to write letters for your mother!" Afterwards when I came home, I found out the reason and proposed to explain the matter, but Yün stopped me, saying, "I would rather be blamed by father than incur the displeasure of mother." And the matter was not cleared up at all.

In the spring of 1790, I again accompanied my father to the magistrate's office at Hankiang [Yangchow]. There was a colleague by the name of Yü Fout'ing, who was staying with his family there. One day, my father said to Fout'ing, "I have been living all my life away from home, and have found it very difficult to find someone to look after my personal comforts. If my son would sympathize with me, he should try to look for one from my home district, so that there will be no dialect difficulty."

　孚亭转述于余，密札致芸，倩媒物色，得姚氏女。芸以成否未定，未即禀知吾母。其来也，托言邻女之嬉游者。及吾父命余接取至署，芸又听旁人意见，托言吾父素所合意者。吾母见之曰："此邻女之嬉游者也，何娶之乎？"芸遂并失爱于姑矣。

　壬子春，余馆真州。吾父病于邗江，余往省，亦病焉。余弟启堂时亦随侍。芸来书曰："启堂弟曾向邻妇借贷，倩芸作保，现追索甚急。"余询启堂，启堂转以嫂氏为多事。余遂批纸尾曰："父子皆病，无钱可偿；俟启堂弟归时，自行打算可也。"

Fout'ing passed on the word to me, and I secretly wrote to Yün, asking her to look round for a girl. She did, and found one of the Yao clan. As Yün was not quite sure whether my father would take her or not, she did not tell mother about it. When the girl was leaving, she merely referred to her as a girl in the neighbourhood who was going for a pleasure trip. After learning, however, that my father had instructed me to bring the girl to his quarters for good, she listened to someone's advice and invented the story that this was the girl my father had had in mind for a long time. "But you said she was going for a pleasure trip! Now why does he marry her?" remarked my mother. And so Yün incurred my mother's displeasure, too.

I was working at Chenchow [Icheng, Kiangsu] in the spring of 1792. My father happened to be ill at Yangchow, and when I went there to see him, I fell ill, too. At that time, my younger brother Ch'it'ang was also there, attending on my father. In her letter to me, Yün mentioned that Ch'it'ang had borrowed some money from a woman neighbour for which she was the guarantor, and that now the creditor was pressing for repayment. I asked Ch'it'ang about it, and he was rather displeased, thinking that Yün was meddling with his affairs. So I merely wrote a postscript at the end of a letter with the words: "Both father and son are sick and we have no money to pay the loan. Wait till younger brother comes home, and let him take care of it himself."

　　未几，病皆愈，余仍往真州。芸覆书来，吾父拆视之，中述启弟
邻项事，且云："令堂以老人之病皆由姚姬而起。翁病稍痊，宜密嘱
姚托言思家，妾当令其家父母到扬接取；实彼此卸责之计也。"吾父
见书怒甚。询启堂以邻项事，答言不知。遂札饬余曰："汝妇背夫借债，
谗谤小叔，且称姑曰'令堂'，翁曰'老人'，悖谬之甚！我已专人持
札回苏斥逐。汝若稍有人心，亦当知过！"余接此札，如闻青天霹雳；
即肃书认罪，觅骑遄归，恐芸之短见也。到家述其本末，而家人乃持
逐书至，历斥多过，言甚决绝。芸泣曰："妾固不合妄言，但阿翁当
恕妇女无知耳。"越数日，吾父又有手谕至，曰："我不为已甚。汝携
妇别居，勿使我见，免我生气足矣。"

Soon both my father and I got well and I left for Chenchow again. Yün's reply came when I was away and was opened by my father. The letter spoke of Ch'it'ang's loan from the neighbouring woman, and besides contained the words, "Your mother thinks that old man's illness is all due to that Yao girl. When he is improving, you should secretly suggest to Yao to say that she is homesick, and I'll ask her parents to come to Yangchow to take her home. In this way we could wash our hands of the matter." When my father saw this, he was furious. He asked Ch'it'ang about the loan and Ch'it'ang declared he knew nothing about it. So my father wrote a note to me, "Your wife borrowed a loan behind your back and spread scandals about your brother. Moreover, she called her mother-in-law 'your mother' and called her father-in-law 'old man.' This is the height of impudence. I have already sent a letter home by a special messenger, ordering her dismissal from home. If you have any conscience at all, you should realize your own fault!" I received this letter like a bolt from the blue, and immediately wrote a letter of apology to him, hired a horse and hurried home, afraid that Yün might commit suicide. I was explaining the whole matter at home, when the family servant arrived with my father's letter, which detailed her various points of misconduct in a most drastic tone. Yün wept and said, "Of course I was wrong to write like that, but father-in-law ought to forgive a woman's ignorance." After a few days, we received another letter from father: "I won't be too harsh on you. You bring Yün along and stay away from home, and do not let me see your face again."

　　乃寄芸于外家，而芸以母亡弟出，不愿往依族中。幸友人鲁半舫闻而怜之，招余夫妇往居其家萧爽楼。越两载，吾父渐知始末。适余自岭南归，吾父自至萧爽楼，谓芸曰："前事我已尽知，汝盍归乎？"余夫妇欣然，仍归故宅，骨肉重圆。岂料又有憨园之孽障耶！

　　芸素有血疾，以其弟克昌出亡不返，母金氏复念子病没，悲伤过甚所致；自识憨园，年余未发，余方幸其得良药。而憨为有力者夺去，以千金作聘，且许养其母，佳人已属沙叱利矣。

It was proposed then that Yün might stay at her maiden home, but her mother was dead and her younger brother had run away from home, and she was not willing to go and be a dependent on her kinsfolk. Fortunately, my friend Lu Panfang heard of the matter and took pity on us, and asked us to go and stay in his home called Hsiaoshuanglou. After two years had passed, my father began to know the whole truth. It happened that shortly after I returned from Lingnan [in Kwangtung], my father personally came to the Hsiaoshuanglou and said to Yün, "Now I understand everything. Why not come home?" Accordingly we returned happily to the old home and the family was reunited. Who would suspect that the affair of Hanyüan was still brewing ahead!

Yün used to have woman's troubles, with discharges of blood. The ailment developed as a consequence of her brother K'ehch'ang running away from home and her mother dying of grief over it which affected Yün's health very much. Since coming to know Hanyüan, however, the trouble had left her for over a year and I was congratulating myself that this friendship proved better than all medicine. Then Han was married to an influential person, who had offered a thousand dollars for her and, furthermore, undertook to support her mother. "The beauty had therefore fallen into the hands of a barbarian."

余知之而未敢言也。及芸往探始知之，归而呜咽，谓余曰："初不料憨之薄情乃尔也！"

余曰："卿自情痴耳。此中人何情之有哉！况锦衣玉食者未必能安于荆钗布裙也。与其后悔，莫若无成。"

因抚慰之再三。而芸终以受愚为恨，血疾大发。床席支离，刀圭无效。时发时止，骨瘦形销。不数年而逋负日增，物议日起。老亲又以盟妓一端，憎恶日甚。余则调停中立，已非生人之境矣。

芸生一女，名青君。时年十四，颇知书，且极贤能，质钗典服，幸赖辛劳。子名逢森，时年十二，从师读书。

I had known of this for some time, but dared not mention it to Yün. However, she went to see her one day and learnt the news for herself. On coming back, she told me amidst sobs, "I did not think that Han could be so heartless!"

"You yourself are crazy," I said. "What do you expect of a sing-song girl? Besides, one who is used to beautiful dresses and nice food like her will hardly be satisfied with the lot of a poor housewife. It were better like this than to marry her and find it to one's cost afterwards."

I tried my best to comfort her, but Yün could never quite recover from the shock of being betrayed and her troubles came again. She was confined to bed and no medicine was of any avail. The illness then became chronic and she grew greatly emaciated. After a few years, our debts piled up higher and higher, and people began to make unpleasant remarks. My parents also began to dislike her more and more on account of the fact that she had been a sworn sister to a sing-song girl. I was placed in an embarrassing position between my parents and wife and from that time on, I did not know what human happiness was.

Yün had given birth to a daughter, named Ch'ingchün, who was then fourteen years old. She knew how to read, and being a very understanding child, quietly went through the hardships with us, often undertaking the pawning of jewelleries and clothing. We had also a son named Fengsen, who was then twelve and was studying under a private tutor.

　　余连年无馆，设一书画铺于家门之内。三日所进，不敷一日所出，焦劳困苦，竭蹶时形。隆冬无裘，挺身而过。青君亦衣单股栗，犹强曰"不寒"。因是芸誓不医药。

　　偶能起床，适余有友人周春煦自福郡王幕中归，倩人绣《心经》一部。芸念绣经可以消灾降福，且利其绣价之丰，竟绣焉。而春煦行色匆匆，不能久待，十日告成。弱者骤劳，致增腰酸头晕之疾。岂知命薄者，佛亦不能发慈悲也！绣经之后，芸病转增，唤水索汤，上下厌之。

I was out of job for several years, and had set up a shop for selling books and paintings in my own home. The income of the shop for three days was hardly sufficient to meet one day's expenses, and I was hard pressed for money and worried all the time. I went through the severe winter without a padded gown and Ch'ingchün too was often shivering in her thin dress, but insisted on saying that she did not feel cold at all. For this reason, Yün swore that she would never see any doctor or take any medicine.

It happened once that she could get up from bed, when my friend Chou Ch'unhsü, who had just returned from the yamen of Prince Fu, wanted to pay for someone to embroider a buddhist book, the *Prajnaparamita Sutra*. Yün undertook to do it, being attracted by the handsome remuneration and besides believing that embroidering the text of a buddhist sutra might help to bring good luck and ward off calamities. My friend, however, was in a hurry to depart and could not wait a little longer, and Yün finished it in ten days. Such work was naturally too much of a strain for a person in her state, and she began to complain of dizziness and back-ache. How did I know that even Buddha would not show mercy to a person born under an evil star! Her illness then became very much aggravated after embroidering the buddhist sutra. She needed more attention and wanted now tea and now medicine, and the people in the family began to feel weary of her.

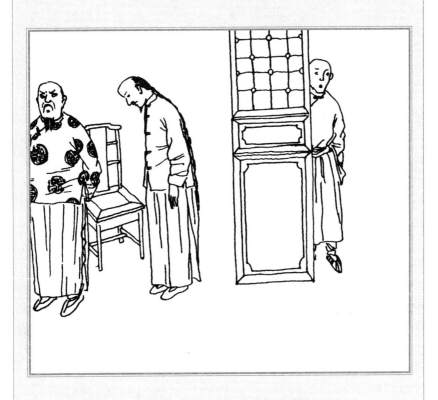

　　有西人赁屋于余画铺之左，放利债为业，时倩余作画，因识之。友人某向渠借五十金，乞余作保，余以情有难却，允焉。而某竟挟资远遁。西人惟保是问，时来饶舌，初以笔墨为抵，渐至无物可偿。岁底吾父家居，西人索债，咆哮于门。吾父闻之，召余呵责曰："我辈衣冠之家，何得负此小人之债！"正剖诉间，适芸有自幼同盟姊适锡山华氏，知其病，遣人问讯。堂上误以为憨园之使，因愈怒曰："汝妇不守闺训，结盟娼妓。汝亦不思习上，滥伍小人。若置汝死地，情有不忍，姑宽三日限，速自为计，迟必首汝逆矣！"

There was a Shansi man who had rented a house on the left of my art shop, and used to lend money at high interest for his living. He often asked me to do some painting for him, and in this way came to know me. There was a friend of mine who wanted to borrow fifty dollars from him and asked me to guarantee the loan. I could not refuse him and consented, but my friend eventually ran away with the money. The creditor, of course, came to me as the guarantor for the money, and made a lot of fuss about it. At first, I tried to pay back a part of the loan with my painting, but finally I just had nothing left to offer him in place of cash. At the end of the year, my father came home, and one day the creditor was creating a lot of noise in the house, demanding repayment of the loan. He called me to him and scolded me, saying, "We belong to a scholars' family; how could we fail to repay a loan from such common people?" While I was trying to explain the matter, there appeared a messenger from Mrs. Hua, a childhood friend of Yün's, who had heard about her illness and had sent him to inquire after her health. My father thought that this messenger was from the sing-song girl Han, and became still more infuriated. "Your wife does not cultivate the feminine virtues, but has become sworn sister to a sing-song girl. You yourself do not associate with good friends, but go about with low-down people. I cannot bear to put you to death, but will allow you three days. Make up your own mind what you are going to do in the meantime, or else I will prosecute you at court for filial impiety!"

芸闻而泣曰："亲怒如此，皆我罪孽。妾死君行，君必不忍；妾留君去，君必不舍。姑密唤华家人来，我强起问之。"

因令青君扶至房外，呼华使问曰："汝主母特遣来耶？抑便道来耶？"曰："主母久闻夫人卧病，本欲亲来探望，因从未登门，不敢造次；临时嘱咐，倘夫人不嫌乡居简亵，不妨到乡调养，践幼时灯下之言。"盖芸与同绣日，曾有疾病相扶之誓也。

因嘱之曰："烦汝速归，禀知主母，于两日后放舟密来。"

When Yün heard of this, she wept and said, "It is all my fault that we have displeased our parents. I know that if I kill myself so that you may go, you will not be able to bear my death, and if we separate, you will not be able to bear the parting. Let's ask Mrs. Hua's servant to come in, and I will try to get up from bed and have a talk with him."

She then asked Ch'ingchün to assist her to get up and escort her outside her bedroom, where she asked the messenger from Mrs. Hua whether his mistress had sent him specially to enquire after her illness, or he was merely taking a message on his way. "My mistress has long heard of your illness," replied the servant, "and was thinking of coming personally to see you, but refrained because she thought she had never been here before. When I was leaving, she told me to say that if you do not mind living in a poor country home, she would like you to come to her place to recuperate, in order to fulfil a pledge of hers with you in her childhood days." The messenger was referring to a girlhood pledge between Yün and Mrs. Hua, when they were doing embroidery work together under the same lamplight, that they should assist each other in sickness or trouble.

"You go back quickly then, and tell your mistress to send a boat secretly for us within two days," she instructed the servant.

　　其人既退，谓余曰："华家盟姊情逾骨肉，君若肯至其家，不妨同行；但儿女携之同往既不便，留之累亲又不可，必于两日内安顿之。"

　　时余有表兄王荩臣一子名韫石，愿得青君为媳妇。芸曰："闻王郎懦弱无能，不过守成之子，而王又无成可守；幸诗礼之家，且又独子，许之可也。"余谓荩臣曰："吾父与君有渭阳之谊，欲媳青君，谅无不允。但待长而嫁，势所不能。余夫妇往锡山后，君即禀知堂上，先为童媳，何如？"荩臣喜曰："谨如命。"逢森亦托友人夏揖山转荐学贸易。

When the man had retired from the interview with her, she said to me, "You know that Mrs. Hua is as good to me as to her own sister and she won't at all mind your coming along too. As for the children, I am afraid that it will be inconvenient for us to bring them along or to leave them here to trouble our parents. I think we must make some arrangements for them within these two days."

There was a cousin of mine (the son of my paternal aunt), by the name of Wang Chinch'en, who had a son called Yünshih, for whom he wished to secure the hand of my daughter. "I hear," said Yün, "that this son of Wang's is rather weak and useless. At best, he would be good only for carrying on, but not for building up a family fortune, but there is no fortune in the family for him to carry on. However, they are a scholars' family and he is the only son. I don't mind giving Ch'ingchün to him." So I said to Chinch'en, "We are cousins, and, of course, I should be glad to give Ch'ingchün to your son, but I am afraid it is difficult under the circumstances for us to keep her until she should grow up. I propose, therefore, that you bring the matter up to my parents after we have gone to Hsishan, and take her over as your 'child daughter-in-law.' I wonder what you think of it?" Chinch'en was very pleased and agreed to my suggestion. As for my son Fengsen, I also asked a friend of mine by the name of Hsia Yishan to place him in a shop as an apprentice.

　　安顿已定，华舟适至。时庚申之腊廿五日也。芸曰："子然出门，不惟招邻里笑，且西人之项无着，恐亦不放，必于明日五鼓悄然而去。"

　　余曰："卿病中能冒晓寒耶？"

　　芸曰："死生有命，无多虑也。"

　　密禀吾父，亦以为然。是夜先将半肩行李挑下船，令逢森先卧。青君泣于母侧。芸嘱曰："汝母命苦，兼亦情痴，故遭此颠沛。幸汝父待我厚，此去可无他虑。两三年内，必当布置重圆。汝至汝家，须尽妇道，勿似汝母。汝之翁姑以得汝为幸，必善视汝。所留箱笼什物，尽付汝带去。汝弟年幼，故未令知。临行时托言就医，数日即归；俟我去远，告知其故，禀闻祖父可也。"

As soon as these arrangements had been made, Mrs. Hua's boat arrived. This was on the twenty-fifth of the twelfth moon, 1800. "If we should leave like this," said Yün, "I am afraid the neighbours will laugh at us, and besides, we haven't repaid the loan due to the Shansi man. I don't think he will let us off. We must leave quietly before dawn tomorrow."

"But can you stand the early damp morning weather in your present state of health?" I asked.

"Oh! I shouldn't worry about that," she said. "It's all a matter of fate how long one is going to live!"

I secretly informed my father about this arrangement, which he also thought best. That night, I first brought a little bag down to the boat and asked Fengsen to go to bed first. Ch'ingchün was weeping by her mother's side, and this was Yün's parting instruction to her: "Mamma was born under an evil star and is, besides, sentimentally passionate. That is why we've come to this. However, your father is very kind to me and you have nothing to worry on my account. I am sure that, in two or three years, we shall be able to manage so that we can be reunited. When you go to your new home, you must try to be a better daughter-in-law than your mother. I know that your parents-in-law will be very kind to you because they are very proud of this match. Whatever we have left behind in the trunks and bags are yours, and you can bring them along. Your younger brother is still young, and therefore we have not let him know. At the time of parting, we are going to say that mamma is going away to see a doctor and will return in a few days. You can explain the whole thing to him when we have gone a long distance, and just let grandfather take care of him."

　　旁有旧妪，即前卷中曾赁其家消暑者，愿送至乡；故是时陪侍在侧，拭泪不已。将交五鼓，暖粥共啜之。芸强颜笑曰："昔一粥而聚，今一粥而散；若作传奇，可名'吃粥记'矣。"逢森闻声亦起，呻曰："母何为？"

　　芸曰："将出门就医耳。"

　　逢森曰："起何早？"

　　曰："路远耳。汝与姊相安在家，毋讨祖母嫌。我与汝父同往，数日即归。"

　　鸡声三唱，芸含泪扶妪，启后门将出，逢森忽大哭，曰："噫，我母不归矣！"

There was with us at this time an old woman who was the one that had let us her country house, as mentioned in the first chapter. She was willing to accompany us to the country, and was now sitting in the room, silently and continually wiping her tears. In the small hours of the morning, we warmed up some congee and ate it together. Yün forced herself to smile and joke, saying, "We first met round a bowl of congee and now we are parting also round a bowl of congee. If someone were to write a play about it, it should be entitled, 'The Romance of the Congee.'" Fengsen heard these words in his sleep, woke up and asked, while yawning:

"What is mamma doing?"

"Mamma is going to see a doctor," Yün replied.

"But why so early?"

"Because the place is so far away. You stay at home with sister and be a good boy and don't annoy grandmother. I am going away with papa and shall be home within a few days."

When the cock had crowed three times, Yün, buried in tears and supported by the old woman, was going out by the back door, when Fengsen suddenly wept aloud and cried: "I know mamma is not coming back!"

　　青君恐惊人，急掩其口而慰之。当是时，余两人寸肠已断，不能复作一语，但止以"勿哭"而已。青君闭门后，芸出巷十数步，已疲不能行，使妪提灯，余背负之而行。将至舟次，几为逻者所执，幸老妪认芸为病女，余为婿，且得舟子（皆华氏工人）闻声接应，相扶下船。解维后，芸始放声痛哭。是行也，其母子已成永诀矣！

　　华名大成，居无锡之东高山，面山而居，躬耕为业，人极朴诚。其妻夏氏，即芸之盟姊也。是日午未之交，始抵其家。华夫人已倚门而待，率两小女至舟，相见甚欢。扶芸登岸，款待殷勤。四邻妇人孺子哄然入室，将芸环视，有相问讯者，有相怜惜者，交头接耳，满屋啾啾。

Ch'ingchün hushed him up, afraid that the noise might wake up other people, and patted him. All this time, Yün and I felt as if our bowels were torn to shreds and we could not say a single word except asking him to stop crying. After Ch'ingchün had closed the door on us, Yün walked along for just about a dozen paces and found she could no more, and I carried her on my back, while the old woman carried the lantern before us. We were almost arrested by a night sentinel when coming near the river, but luckily through the old woman's ruse, Yün passed off as her sick daughter, and I her son-in-law. The boatmen, who were all servants of the Hua family, came to the rescue and helped us down to the boat. When the boat was untied and we were moving, Yün broke down completely and wept bitterly aloud. Actually, mother and son never saw each other again.

Mr. Hua, whose name was Tach'eng, was living on the Tungkao Hill at Wusih, in a house facing the hillside. He tilled the field himself and was a very simple, honest soul. Mrs. Hua, whose family name was Hsia, was, as I have mentioned, Yün's sworn sister. We arrived that day at their home about one o'clock. Mrs. Hua came with her two little daughters to the boat to meet us, and we were all very happy to see each other. She supported Yün up the river bank to her home and gave us a most cordial welcome. The neighbouring women and children all came crowding into the house to look at Yün, some enquiring for news and some expressing their sympathy with her, so that the whole house was full of their twitter.

　　芸谓华夫人曰：“今日真如渔父入桃源矣。”

　　华曰：“妹莫笑。乡人少所见多所怪耳。”

　　自此相安度岁。至元宵，仅隔两旬，而芸渐能起步。是夜观龙灯于打麦场中，神情态度渐可复元。余乃心安，与之私议曰：

　　“我居此非计。欲他适，而短于资，奈何？”

　　芸曰：“妾亦筹之矣。君姊丈范惠来现于靖江盐公堂司会计，十年前曾借君十金，适数不敷，妾典钗凑之。君忆之耶？”

　　余曰：“忘之矣。”

"Now I really feel like the fisherman who went up to the Peach-Blossom Spring,"[1] said Yün to Mrs. Hua.

"I hope sister won't mind these people. The country folk are merely curious."

And so we lived at the place very happily and passed the New Year there. Hardly twenty days had passed since our arrival when the festival of the fifteenth day of the first moon came and Yün was already able to leave her bed. That night we watched a dragon lantern show in a big yard for threshing wheat, and I noticed that Yün was gradually becoming her normal self again. I felt very happy and secretly discussed our future plans with her.

"I don't think we ought to be staying here for ever, but, on the other hand, we have no money to go elsewhere. What shall we do?" I said.

"Your wife has thought about it too," said Yün. "I have an idea. You know the husband of your sister, Mr. Fan Hueilai, is now serving as treasurer in the Salt Bureau of Tsingkiang [in Kiangsu]. Do you remember that, ten years ago, we lent him ten dollars, and it happened that we did not have sufficient money and I pawned my hair-pin to make up the amount?"

"Why, I'd forgotten all about it!" I replied.

---

[1] Reference to an idyllic retreat mentioned in an essay by T'ao Yüanming. — *Tr.*

芸曰："闻靖江去此不远，君盍一往?"

余如其言。时天颇暖，织绒袍哔叽短褂，犹觉其热。此辛酉正月十六日也。是夜宿锡山客旅，赁被而卧。晨起，趁江阴航船，一路逆风，继以微雨。夜至江阴江口，春寒彻骨，沽酒御寒，囊为之罄。踌躇终夜，拟卸衬衣质钱而渡。

十九日，北风更烈，雪势犹浓，不禁惨然泪落。暗计房资渡费，不敢再饮。正心寒股栗间，忽见一老翁，草鞋毡笠，负黄包入店，以目视余，似相识者。

余曰："翁非泰州曹姓耶?"

答曰："然。我非公，死填沟壑矣。今小女无恙，时诵公德。不意今日相逢。何逗留于此?"

"Why don't you go and see him? I hear Tsingkiang is only a little way from here," said Yün.

I took her advice and started off on the sixteenth of the first moon in 1801. The weather was quite mild, and one felt too warm even in a velvet gown and a serge jacket. That night I stayed at an inn at Hsishan, and rented some bedding for my bed. Next morning I took a sailing boat for Kiangyin. The wind was against us and there was a slight rain. At night, we arrived at the mouth of the river by Kiangyin. I felt chilled to the bone and bought some wine to warm myself up, in that way spending the last cash I had with me. I lay there the whole night thinking what I should do, rotating in my mind the idea of perhaps pawning my inside jacket in order to get money for the ferry.[1]

On the nineteenth, the north wind became still severer and snow lay about the fields and I shed tears. I calculated the expenses for the room and the ferry boat and dared not buy another drink. While I was shivering both in my body and my heart, suddenly I saw an old man in sandals and a felt hat enter the shop, carrying a yellow bag on his back. He looked at me and seemed to know me.

"Aren't you Mr. Ts'ao of Taichow?" I asked.

"Yes," replied the old man. "Were it not for you, I would have died long ago in the gutter. Now my daughter is still living and quite well, and she remembers you with gratitude all the time. What a pleasant surprise for us to meet here! What has brought you to this place?"

[1] Kiangyin is on the south bank of the Yangtze. — *Tr.*

　　盖余幕泰州时，有曹姓，本微贱，一女有姿色，已许婿家，有势力者放债谋其女，致涉讼。余从中调护，仍归所许。曹即投入公门为隶，叩首作谢，故识之。余告以投亲遇雪之由。

　　曹曰："明日天晴，我当顺途相送。"出钱沽酒，备极款洽。

　　二十日，晓钟初动，即闻江口唤渡声。余惊起，呼曹同济。曹曰："勿急。宜饱食登舟。"乃代偿房饭钱，拉余出沽。余以连日逗留，即欲赶渡，食不下咽，强啖麻饼两枚。及登舟，江风如箭，四肢发战。

It should be explained that when I was working in the yamen of Taichow ten years ago, there was a Mr. Ts'ao of a humble family who had a beautiful daughter already betrothed to someone, and an influential person had lent him money with the object of obtaining his daughter. In this way he was involved in a lawsuit. I helped him in the affair and managed to return his daughter to the family of the betrothed. Old Ts'ao came to offer his services at the yamen as a token of his gratitude and kowtowed to thank me. That was how I came to know him. I told him how I was on my way to see my brother-in-law and how I had run into the snow.

"If it clears up tomorrow," said Ts'ao, "I shall accompany you, for I am passing that way myself." And he took out some money to buy wine, showing the greatest cordiality toward me.

On the twentieth, as soon as the morning temple bell had struck, I already heard the ferry-man crying at the bank for passengers to come aboard. I got up in a hurry and asked Ts'ao to go together. "No hurry. We must eat something before going down to the boat," said Ts'ao. Then he paid the room and board for me and asked me to go out for a drink. As I had been delayed so long on my way and was anxious to start off, I was in no mood for eating, but merely chewed two pieces of sesame-seed cake. When I got to the boat, there was a piercing wind blowing over the river, and I was shivering all over.

　　曹曰："闻江阴有人缢于靖,其妻雇是舟而往。必俟雇者来始渡耳。"

　　枵腹忍寒,午始解缆。至靖,暮烟四合矣。

　　曹曰："靖有公堂两处。所访者城内耶? 城外耶?"

　　余踉跄随其后,且行且对曰："实不知其内外也。"

　　曹曰："然则且止宿,明日往访耳。"

　　进旅店,鞋袜已为泥淤湿透,索火烘之。草草饮食,疲极酣睡。晨起,袜烧其半。曹又代偿房饭钱。访至城中,惠来尚未起,闻余至,披衣出,见余状惊曰："舅何狼狈至此?"

　　余曰："姑勿问。有银乞借二金,先遣送我者。"

"I am told there is a native of Kiangyin who hanged himself at Tsingkiang, and his wife has engaged this boat to go there," said Ts'ao. "We have to wait till she comes, before we can cross the river."

So I waited there, hungry and cold, till noon before we started off. When we arrived at Tsingkiang, there was already an evening haze lying over the countryside.

"There are two yamen at Tsingkiang, one inside the city and the other outside. Which one is your relative working in?"

"I really don't know," I said, walking dismally behind him.

"In that case, we might just as well stop here and call on him tomorrow," said Ts'ao.

When I entered the inn, my shoes and socks were already drenched through and covered with mud, and I had them dried up before the fire. I was all in, hurried through my meal and dropped into a sound sleep. Next morning when I got up, my socks were half burnt by fire. Ts'ao again paid for my room and board. When I arrived at Hueilai's yamen in the city, he had not got up yet, but hurriedly put on his gown and came out to see me. When he saw the state I was in, he was quite astonished and said, "Why, what's the matter with brother-in-law? You look so shabby!"

"Don't ask me questions. Lend me two dollars first, if you have any with you. I want to pay back a friend who came along with me."

　　惠来以番饼二圆授余，即以赠曹。曹力却，受一圆而去。余乃历述所遭，并言来意。

　　惠来曰："郎舅至戚，即无宿逋，亦应竭尽绵力；无如航海盐船新被盗，正当盘账之时，不能挪移丰赠，当勉措番银二十圆，以偿旧欠，何如？"余本无奢望，遂诺之。留住两日，天已晴暖，即作归计。廿五日，仍回华宅。

　　芸曰："君遇雪乎？"余告以所苦。因惨然曰："雪时，妾以君为抵靖，乃尚逗留江口。幸遇曹老，绝处逢生，亦可谓吉人天相矣。"

　　越数日，得青君信，知逢森已为揖山荐引入店。芝臣请命于吾父，择正月二十四日将伊接去。儿女之事粗能了了，但分离至此，令人终觉惨伤耳。

Hueilai gave me two Mexican dollars which I gave to Ts'ao, but Ts'ao would not take them; only after my insistence did he receive one dollar before going away. I then told Hueilai about all that had happened, as well as the purpose of my visit.

"You know we are brothers-in-law," said Hueilai, "I should help you even if I did not owe you the debt. The trouble is, our salt boats on the sea were recently captured by pirates, and we are still trying to straighten up the accounts, and I am afraid I shan't be able to help you much. Would it be all right if I tried to provide twenty dollars in repayment of the old debt?" As I was not expecting much anyway, I consented. After staying there for two days, the sky had cleared up and the weather became milder and I came home, arriving at Mrs. Hua's house on the twenty-fifth.

"Did you run into the snow on the way?" inquired Yün. I told her what had happened on the way and she remarked sadly, "When it snowed, I thought you had already arrived at Tsingkiang, but you were then still on the river! It was very lucky of you to have met old Ts'ao. Really Heaven always provides for good people."

After a few days, we received a letter from Ch'ingchün informing us that her younger brother had already found a job as apprentice through the good offices of my friend Yishan. Ch'ingchün herself was also brought to Chinch'en's home on the twenty-fourth of the first moon, with the permission of my father. Thus my children's affairs were all settled, but it was hard for parents and children to part like this.

　　二月初，日暖风和，以靖江之项薄备行装，访故人胡肯堂于邗江盐署。有贡局众司事公延入局，代司笔墨，身心稍定。至明年壬戌八月，接芸书曰："病体全瘳。惟寄食于非亲非友之家，终觉非久长之策，愿亦来邗，一睹平山之胜。"余乃赁屋于邗江先春门外，临河两椽。自至华氏接芸同行。华夫人赠一小奚奴曰阿双，帮司炊爨，并订他年结邻之约。时已十月，平山凄冷，期以春游。

　　满望散心调摄，徐图骨肉重圆。不满月，而贡局司事忽裁十有五人，余系友中之友，遂亦散闲。芸始犹百计代余筹画，强颜慰藉，未尝稍涉怨尤。

The weather was clear and mild at the beginning of the second moon. With the money I had obtained from my brother-in-law, I made arrangements for a trip to Yangchow, where my old friend Hu K'engt'ang was working at the Salt Bureau. I obtained a post there as secretary at the imperial tax bureau and felt more settled. In the eighth moon of the following year, 1802, I received a letter from Yün which said: "I have completely recovered now. I don't think it is right for me to be staying at a friend's place for ever, and wish very much to come to Yangchow, and see the famous P'ingshan." I then rented a two-roomed house on a river outside the First-in-Spring Gate of Yangchow City, and went personally to bring Yün to our new home. Mrs. Hua presented us with a little boy servant, called Ah Shuang, who was to help us in cooking and general housework. She also made an agreement with us that some day we should live together as neighbours. As it was already in the tenth moon and it was too cold at P'ingshan, we had to put off our visit there until next spring.

I was fully hoping, then, that we were going to have a quiet life and Yün's health would steadily recover and that eventually we might be reunited with our family. In less than a month, however, the yamen was reducing its staff and cut fifteen persons. As I was only indirectly recommended by a friend, naturally I was among those sent away. Yün at first thought of different plans for me; she tried to be cheerful and comforted me, and never said a word of complaint.

　　至癸亥仲春，血疾大发。余欲再至靖江，作"将伯"之呼。

　　芸曰："求亲不如求友。"

　　余曰："此言虽是，奈友虽关切，现皆闲处，自顾不遑。"

　　芸曰："幸天时已暖，前途可无阻雪之虑。愿君速去速回，勿以病人为念。君或体有不安，妾罪更重矣。"

　　时已薪水不继，余佯为雇骡以安其心，实则囊饼徒步，且食且行。向东南，两渡叉河，约八九十里，四望无村落。至更许，但见黄沙漠漠，明星闪闪，得一土地祠，高约五尺许，环以短墙，植以双柏。因向神叩首，祝曰："苏州沈某投亲失路至此，欲假神祠一宿，幸神怜佑！"

Thus we dragged on till the second moon of 1803, when she had a severe relapse, with profuse discharges of blood. I wanted to go again to Tsingkiang for help, but Yün said:

"It is better to go to a friend than to a relative for help."

"You are quite right," I said, "but all my friends are themselves in trouble and won't be able to help us, however kind they are."

"All right, then," she said. "The weather is quite mild now and I don't think there will be any snow. Go quickly and come back quickly, but don't worry on my account. Take good care of yourself and increase not the burden of my sins."

At this time, we were already unable to meet our daily expenses, but in order to ease her mind, I pretended to her that I was going to hire a donkey. As a matter of fact, I took the journey on foot, merely eating some wheat cakes in my pocket whenever I felt hungry. I went in a southeasterly direction and crossed two creeks. After going for eighty or ninety *li*, I found a deserted country without any houses around. As night came, I saw only a stretch of yellow sands under the starry sky. There I found a little shrine of the God of Earth, about over five feet high, enclosed by a low wall, with two little cypress trees in front. Then I kowtowed to the God and prayed: "I am Mr. Shen of Soochow on my way to a relative's. I've lost my bearings and intend to borrow thy temple to pass a night here. Mayst thou protect me!"

于是移小石香炉于旁，以身探之，仅容半体，以风帽反戴掩面，坐半身于中，出膝于外，闭目静听，微风萧萧而已。足疲神倦，昏然睡去。

及醒，东方已白，短墙外忽有步语声。急出探视，盖土人赶集经此也。问以途，曰："南行十里即泰兴县城，穿城向东南，十里一土墩，过八墩，即靖江，皆康庄也。"余乃反身，移炉于原位，叩首作谢而行。过泰兴，即有小车可附。

申刻抵靖，投刺焉。良久，司阍者曰："范爷因公往常州去矣。"察其辞色，似有推托。余诘之曰："何日可归？"

I then put away the little stone incense tripod and tried to crawl in. The shrine, however, was too small for my body by half and I managed to sit on the ground, leaving my legs outside. I turned my travelling cap round, using the back to cover my face, and thus sat there listening with my eyes closed, but all I could hear was the whistling of winds blowing by. My feet were sore and my spirit was tired and soon I dozed off.

When I woke up, it was already broad daylight and suddenly I heard people's footsteps and sounds of talking outside the low enclosure. Immediately I peeped out and saw that it was the peasants, who were going to a fair, passing by. I asked them for directions and they told me that I was to go straight south for ten *li* until I should reach Taihing City, and after going through the city, to go southeast for ten *li* until I should come across an earthen mound; after passing eight such mounds, I would then arrive at Tsingkiang. All I had to do was to follow the main road. I turned back then, put the incense tripod back in its original place, thanked the God for the night's rest and started off. After passing Taihing, I took a wheel-barrow and arrived at Tsingkiang about four o'clock in the afternoon.

I sent in my card and waited for a long time before the watchman came out and said, "Mr. Fan is away on official business to Ch'angchow." From the way he talked, I thought this was merely a pretext for not seeing me. I asked him when his master was coming home.

曰："不知也。"

余曰："虽一年亦将待之。"

阍者会余意，私问曰："公与范爷嫡郎舅耶？"

余曰："苟非嫡者，不待其归矣。"

阍者曰："公姑待之。"越三日，乃以回靖告，共挪二十五金。雇
骡急返。

芸正形容惨变，咻咻涕泣。见余归，卒然曰："君知昨午阿双卷
逃乎？倩人大索，今犹不得。失物小事；人系伊母临行再三交托，今
若逃归，中有大江之阻，已觉堪虞。倘其父母匿子图诈，将奈之何？
且有何颜见我盟姊！"

"I don't know," replied the servant.

"Then I am going to stay here until he returns, even if I have to wait a year."

The watchman guessed the purpose of my visit and secretly asked me, "Is Mrs. Fan really your own sister by the same mother?"

"If she weren't my own sister, I wouldn't have decided to wait until Mr. Fan's return."

The watchman then asked me to stay. After three days, I was told that Mr. Fan had returned and was given twenty-five dollars, with which I hurriedly hired a donkey and returned home.

I found Yün very sad and sobbing at home. When she saw me, she said rather abruptly, "Do you know that Ah Shuang ran away yesterday with our things? I have asked people to go about looking for him, but so far with no results. I don't mind losing the things, but the boy was given to me by his own mother, who told me repeatedly on parting to take good care of him. If he is running home, he will have to cross the Yangtze River, and I don't know what may happen to him. Or if his parents should hide him away and ask me for their son, what are we to do? And how am I going to face my sworn sister?"

　　余曰："请勿急。卿虑过深矣。匪子图诈，诈其富有也；我夫妇两肩担一口耳。况携来半载，授衣分食，从未稍加扑责，邻里咸知。此实小奴丧良，乘危窃逃。华家盟姊赠以匪人，彼无颜见卿；卿何反谓无颜见彼耶？今当一面呈县立案，以杜后患可也。"

　　芸闻余言，意似稍释；然自此梦中呓语，时呼"阿双逃矣！"或呼"憨何负我！"病势日以增矣。

　　余欲延医诊治。芸阻曰："妾病始因弟亡母丧，悲痛过甚；继为情感；后由忿激。而平素又多过虑，满望努力做一好媳妇而不能得，以至头眩、怔忡诸症毕备。所谓病入膏肓，良医束手，请勿为无益之费。

"Please calm yourself," I said. "I think there is no ground for such anxiety. One who hides away his own son must do it for blackmail, but they know perfectly well that we haven't got any money. Besides, since the boy's coming here half a year ago, we have given him food and clothing, and have never struck him or been harsh to him, as everybody round here knows. I think the real fact is that the boy was a rascal and, seeing that we were in a bad way, stole our things and ran away. As for Mrs. Hua, it is she, rather than you, that should feel uneasy—for sending you such a scamp. The thing to do is for us to report the matter immediately to the magistrate, and prevent any future complications."

Yün felt a little easier after hearing my view of the situation, but from then on she often cried out in her sleep "Ah Shuang has run away!" or "How could Han be so heartless!" and her illness became worse and worse every day. I wanted to send for a doctor, but Yün stopped me saying:

"You know my illness started in consequence of deep grief over my mother's death following upon K'ehch'ang's running away, then it was aggravated through my passion for Han and finally made worse by my chagrin at this recent affair. Besides, I was often too cautious and afraid of making mistakes. I have tried my best to be a good daughter-in-law, but have failed, and have consequently developed dizziness and palpitation of the heart. The illness is now deep in my system and no doctor will be of any avail, and you may just as well spare yourself the expense.

　　"忆妾唱随二十三年，蒙君错爱，百凡体恤，不以顽劣见弃。知
己如君，得婿如此，妾已此生无憾。若布衣暖，菜饭饱，一室雍雍，
优游泉石，如沧浪亭、萧爽楼之处境，真成烟火神仙矣。神仙几世才
能修到，我辈何人，敢望神仙耶！强而求之，致于造物之忌，即有情
魔之扰。总因君太多情，妾生薄命耳！"

　　因又呜咽而言曰："人生百年，终归一死。今中道相离，忽焉长别，
不能终奉箕帚，目睹逢森娶妇，此心实觉耿耿。"言已，泪落如豆。
余勉强慰之曰："卿病八年，恹恹欲绝者屡矣。今何忽作断肠语耶？"

As I look back upon the twenty-three years of our married life, I know that you have loved me and been most considerate to me, in spite of all my faults. I am happy to die with a husband and understanding friend like you and I have no regrets. Yes, I have been as happy as a fairy at times, with my warm cotton clothing and frugal but full meals and the happy home we had. Do you remember how we used to enjoy ourselves amongst springs and rocks, as at the Ts'anglang Pavilion and the Hsiaoshuanglou? But who are we to enjoy the good luck of a fairy, of which only those are worthy who have lived a virtuous life from incarnation to incarnation? We had, therefore, offended the Creator by trying to snatch a happiness that was above our lot; hence our various earthly troubles. It all comes of your too great love, bestowed upon one who is ill-fated and unworthy of this happiness."

After a while she spoke again amidst sobs, "Every one has to die once. My only regret is, we have to part half-way from each other for ever, and I am not able to be your wife until the end of your days and see with my own eyes the wedding of Fengsen." After saying this, tears rolled down her cheeks as big as peas. I tried to comfort her by saying, "You have been ill for eight years, and this is not the first time that you are in a critical condition. Why do you suddenly say such heart-breaking words?"

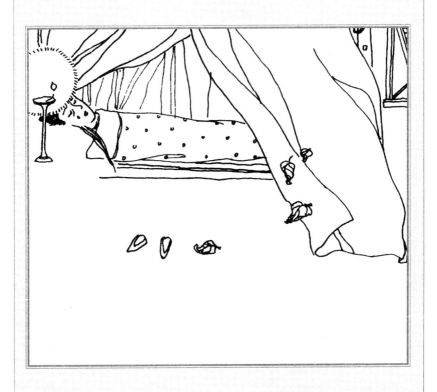

芸曰："连日梦我父母放舟来接，闭目即飘然上下，如行云雾中，殆魂离而躯壳存乎？"

余曰："此神不收舍，服以补剂，静心调养，自能安痊。"

芸又歔欷曰："妾若稍有生机一线，断不敢惊君听闻。今冥路已近，苟再不言，言无日矣。君之不得亲心，流离颠沛，皆由妾故。妾死则亲心自可挽回，君亦可免牵挂。堂上春秋高矣，妾死，君宜早归。如无力携妾骸骨归，不妨暂厝于此，待君将来可耳。愿君另续德容兼备者，以奉双亲，抚我遗子，妾亦瞑目矣。"言至此，痛肠欲裂，不觉惨然大恸。

余曰："卿果中道相舍，断无再续之理。况'曾经沧海难为水，除却巫山不是云'耳。"

"I have been dreaming lately," she said, "of my parents who have sent a boat to welcome me home. Whenever I close my eyes, I feel my body is so light, so light, like one walking among the clouds. It seems that my spirit has already departed and only my body remains."

"This is the effect of your extreme weakness," I said. "If you will take some tonic and rest yourself properly, I am sure you will get well."

Then Yün sighed again and said, "If there were the slightest ray of hope, I would not have told you all these things. But now death is approaching and it is high time I spoke my mind. I know you have displeased your parents all on my account; therefore when I die, your parents' attitude will change round, and you yourself will feel more at ease toward your parents. You know they are already very old, and when I die, you should return to them as soon as possible. If you cannot bring my remains back to the native district for burial, you can temporarily keep my coffin here and then see to its removal afterwards. I hope you will find another one who is both beautiful and good to take my place and serve our parents and bring up my children, and then I shall die content." At this point, she broke down completely and fell to weeping as if her bowels had been cut through.

"Even if you should leave me half-way like this," I said, "I shall never marry again. Besides, 'it is difficult to be water for one who has seen the great seas, and difficult to be clouds for one who has seen the Yangtze Gorges.' "

　　芸乃执余手而更欲有言，仅断续叠言"来世"二字。忽发喘口噤，两目瞪视；千呼万唤，已不能言。痛泪两行，泫泫流溢。既而喘渐微，泪渐干，一灵缥缈，竟尔长逝。时嘉庆癸亥三月三十日也。当是时，孤灯一盏，举目无亲，两手空拳，寸心欲碎。绵绵此恨，曷其有极！

　　承吾友胡肯堂以十金为助，余尽室中所有，变卖一空，亲为成殓。

　　呜呼！芸一女流，具男子之襟怀才识。归吾门后，余日奔走衣食，中馈缺乏，芸能纤悉不介意。及余家居，惟以文字相辩析而已。卒之疾病颠连，赍恨以没，谁致之耶？余有负闺中良友，又何可胜道哉！奉劝世间夫妇，固不可彼此相仇，亦不可过于情笃。语云："恩爱夫妻不到头。"如余者，可作前车之鉴也。

Then Yün held my hand and was going to say something again, but she could only mumble the words "Next incarnation!" half audibly again and again. Suddenly she began to feel short of breath, her chin was set, her eyes stared wide open, and however I called her name, she could not utter a single word. Two lines of tears kept on rolling down her cheeks. After a while, her breath became weaker, her tears gradually dried up and her spirit departed from this life for ever. This was on the thirtieth of the third moon, 1803. A solitary lamp was shining then in the room, and a sense of utter forlornness overcame me. In my heart opened a wound that shall be healed nevermore!

My friend Hu K'engt'ang kindly helped me with ten dollars, and together with this and what I could obtain by selling all I had in the house, I saw to her proper burial.

Alas! Yün was a woman with the heart and talent of a man. From the time she was married into my home, I had been forced to run about abroad for a living, while she was left without sufficient money, and she never said a word of complaint. When I could stay at home, our sole occupation was the discussion of books and literature. She died in poverty and sickness without being able to see her own children, and who was to blame but myself? How could I ever express the debt I owe to a good chamber companion? I should like to urge upon all married couples in the world neither to hate nor to be too passionately attached to each other. As the proverb says, "A loving couple could never reach grand old age together." Mine is a case in point.

　　回煞之期，俗传是日魂必随煞而归，故房中铺设一如生前，且须铺生前旧衣于床上，置旧鞋于床下，以待魂归瞻顾。吴下相传谓之"收眼光"；延羽士作法，先召于床而后遣之，谓之"接眚"。邗江俗例，设酒肴于死者之室，一家尽出，谓之"避眚"；以故有因避被窃者。芸娘眚期，房东因同居而出避，邻家嘱余亦设肴远避。余冀魂归一见，姑漫应之。同乡张禹门谏余曰："因邪入邪，宜信其有，勿尝试也。"

　　余曰："所以不避而待之者，正信其有也。"

　　张曰："回煞犯煞，不利生人。夫人即或魂归，业已阴阳有间，窃恐欲见者无形可接，应避者反犯其锋耳。"

According to custom, the spirit of the deceased is supposed to return to the house on a certain day after his death, and people used to arrange the room exactly as the deceased had left it, putting his old clothes on the bed and his old shoes by the bedside for the returning spirit to take a farewell look. We called this in Soochow "closing the spirit's eyes." People also used to invite Taoist monks to recite incantations, calling to the spirit to visit the deathbed and then sending it away. This was called "welcoming the spirit." At Yangchow the custom was to prepare wine and dishes and leave them in the dead man's chamber, while the whole family would go away in order to "avoid the spirit." It often happened that things were stolen while the house was thus deserted. On this day, my landlord, who was staying with me, left the house, and my neighbours urged me to leave the offerings at home and get away also. To this I gave a cold, indifferent reply, for I was hoping to see the spirit of Yün again. There was a certain Chang Yümen of the same district who warned me saying, "One may be very well possessed by the evil spirit, when one's mind dwells on the uncanny. I should not advise you to try it, for I rather believe in the existence of ghosts."

"This is the very reason I am going to stay—because I believe that ghosts do exist," I replied.

"To encounter the spirit of the deceased on its return home has an evil influence on living men," Chang replied. "Even if your wife's spirit should return, she is living in a world different from ours. I am afraid you won't be able to see her form, but will, on the other hand, be affected by her evil influence."

　　时余痴心不昧，强对曰："死生有命。君果关切，伴我何如？"

　　张曰："我当于门外守之。君有异见，一呼即入可也。"

　　余乃张灯入室，见铺设宛然，而音容已杳，不禁心伤泪涌。又恐泪眼模糊，失所欲见，忍泪睁目，坐床而待。抚其所遗旧服，香泽犹存，不觉柔肠寸断，冥然昏去。转念待魂而来，何遽睡耶！开目四视，见席上双烛青焰荧荧，光缩如豆，毛骨悚然，通体寒栗。因摩两手擦额，细瞩之，双焰渐起，高至尺许，纸裱顶格几被所焚。余正得藉光四顾间，光忽又缩如前。

I was so madly in love with her that I did not care. "I don't care a damn about it," I said to him. "If you are so concerned about me, why not stay on and keep me company?"

"I'll stay outside the door. If you should see anything strange, just call for me."

I then went in with a lamp in my hand and saw the room was exactly as she had left it, only my beloved was not there, and tears welled up in my eyes in spite of myself. I was afraid then that with my wet eyes, I should not be able to see her form clearly, and I held back my tears and sat on the bed, waiting for her appearance with wide open eyes. Softly I touched her old dress and smelt the odour of her body which still remained, and was so affected by it that I fainted off. Then I thought to myself, How could I let myself doze off since I was waiting for the return of her spirit? I opened my eyes again and looked round and saw the two candle-lights burning low on the table as small as little peas. It gave me a goose-flesh and I shuddered all over. Then I rubbed my hands and my forehead and looked carefully and saw the pair of candle-lights leapt higher and higher till they were over a foot long and the papered wooden frame of the ceiling was going to catch fire. The sudden glow of the lights illuminated the whole room and enabled me to look round clearly, when suddenly they grew small and dark as before.

　　此时心春股栗，欲呼守者进观；而转念柔魂弱魄，恐为盛阳所逼，悄呼芸名而祝之，满室寂然，一无所见。既而烛焰复明，不复腾起矣。出告禹门，服余胆壮，不知余实一时情痴耳。

　　芸没后，忆和靖"妻梅子鹤"语，自号梅逸。权葬芸于扬州西门外之金桂山，俗呼郝家宝塔。买一棺之地，从遗言寄于此。携木主还乡，吾母亦为悲悼。青君、逢森归来，痛哭成服。

　　启堂进言曰："严君怒犹未息，兄宜仍往扬州。俟严君归里，婉言劝解，再当专札相招。"

At this time I was in a state of excitement and wanted to call in my companion, when I thought that her gentle female spirit might be scared away by the presence of another living man. Secretly and in a quiet tone, I called her name and prayed to her, but the whole room was buried in silence and I could not see a thing. Then the candle-lights grew bright again, but did not shoot high up as before. I went out and told Yümen about it, and he thought me very bold, but did not know that I was merely in love.

After Yün's death, I thought of the poet Lin Hoching who "took the plum-trees for his wives and a stork for his son," and I called myself "Meiyi," meaning "one bereaved of the plum-tree." I provisionally buried Yün on the Golden Cassia Hill outside the West Gate of Yangchow, at the place which was commonly known as "The Precious Pagoda of the Ho Family." I bought a lot and buried her there, according to her dying wish, bringing home with me the wooden tablet for worship. My mother was also deeply touched by the news of her death. Ch'ingchün and Fengsen came home, wept bitterly and went into mourning.

"You know father is still angry with you," said my brother Ch'it'ang. "You'd better stay away at Yangchow for some time and wait till father returns home, when I shall speak for you and then write for you to come home."

　　余遂拜母别子女，痛哭一场；复至扬州，卖画度日。因得常哭于芸娘之墓，影单形双，备极凄凉。且偶经故居，伤心惨目。重阳日，邻家皆黄，芸墓独青。守坟者曰："此好穴场，故地气旺也。"余暗祝曰："秋风已紧，身尚衣单。卿若有灵，佑我图得一馆，度此残年，以待家乡信息。"

　　未几，江都幕客章驭庵先生欲回浙江葬亲，倩余代庖三月，得备卸寒之具。封篆出署，张禹门招寓其家。张亦失馆，度岁艰难，商于余；即以余资二十金倾囊借之，且告曰："此本留为亡荆扶柩之费，一俟得有乡音，偿我可也。"

I then kowtowed to my mother and parted from my daughter and son and wept aloud for a while, before I departed again for Yangchow, where I painted for my living. Thus I was often enabled to loiter round and weep over Yün's grave, forlorn soul that I was! And whenever I passed our old house, the sight was too much for me to bear. On the Double Ninth Festival Day, I found that, while all the other graves were yellow, hers was still green. The graveyard keeper said to me, "This is a propitious place for burial, that is why the spirit of the earth is so strong." And I secretly prayed to her, "O Yün! The autumn wind is blowing high, and my gowns are still thin. If you have any influence, protect me and arrange that I may have a job to pass the end of the year, while waiting abroad for news from home."

Soon afterwards, one Mr. Chang Yü-an, who had a post as secrtary at the Kiangtu [Yangchow] yamen, was going to bury his parents at home in Chekiang, and asked me to take his place for three months. And thus I was provided against the winter. After I left that place, Chang Yümen asked me to stay at his home. He was out of job too, and told me that he was finding it hard to meet the expenses at the end of the year. I gave him all the twenty dollars I had in my pocket, and told him that this was the money I had reserved for bringing Yün's coffin home and that he could pay me back when I heard word from my family.

　　是年即寓张度岁。晨占夕卜，乡音殊杳。至甲子三月，接青君信，知吾父有病，即欲归苏，又恐触旧忿。正趑趄观望间，复接青君信，始痛悉吾父业已辞世，刺骨痛心，呼天莫及。无暇他计，即星夜驰归。触首灵前，哀号流血。呜呼！吾父一生辛苦，奔走于外。生余不肖，既少承欢膝下，又未侍药床前，不孝之罪何可逭哉！

　　吾母见余哭，曰："汝何此日始归耶？"

　　余曰："儿之归，幸得青君孙女信也。"吾母目余弟妇，遂默然。

　　余入幕守灵至七，终无一人以家事告，以丧事商者。余自问人子之道已缺，故亦无颜询问。

So that year I passed the New Year at Chang's home. I was waiting for mail from home morning and night, but no news came at all. In the third moon of 1804, I received a letter from my daughter Ch'ingchün, informing me of my father's illness. I wanted very much to go home to Soochow, but was afraid of arousing father's anger. While I was still hesitating, I received a second letter from her, telling me that father had died. Sorrow went into my heart and pierced my bones and I cried to heaven in vain, for I knew it was too late. Brushing aside all considerations, I dashed home under the starry sky. I wailed bitterly and knocked my head against the coffin until I bled. Alas! my father had a hard time all his life working away from home, and he begot such an unfilial son as I, who was never able to minister to his pleasure while he was alive, nor able to serve him at his death-bed. Great, indeed, is my sin!

"Why didn't you come home earlier then?" asked my mother, seeing me weeping so bitterly.

"Had it not been for Ch'ingchün's letter," I said, "I would not even have heard of it at all." My mother cast a look at my brother's wife and kept silent.

I then kept watch over the coffin in the hall, but throughout the seven weeks for mourning ceremonies, not one in the whole family spoke to me about family affairs or discussed the funeral arrangements with me. I was ashamed of myself for not fulfilling a son's duties and would not ask them questions, either.

　　一日，忽有向余索逋者登门饶舌。余出应曰："欠债不还，固应催索。然吾父骨肉未寒，乘凶追呼，未免太甚。"中有一人私谓余曰："我等皆有人招之使来。公且避出，当向招我者索偿也。"余曰："我欠我偿，公等速退！"皆唯唯而去。

　　余因呼启堂谕之曰："兄虽不肖，并未作恶不端。若言出嗣降服，从未得过纤毫嗣产。此次奔丧归来，本人子之道，岂为争产故耶？大丈夫贵乎自立，我既一身归，仍以一身去耳！"言已，返身入幕，不觉大恸。

　　叩辞吾母，走告青君，行将出走深山，求赤松子于世外矣。青君正劝阻间，友人夏南熏字淡安，夏逢泰字揖山两昆季寻踪而至，抗声谏余曰：

One day some men suddenly appeared at our house to ask for repayment of a loan, and made a lot of noise in the hall. I came out and said to them, "I don't blame you for pressing for repayment of the debt. But isn't it rather mean of you to create such a turmoil, while my father's remains are scarcely cold yet?" One among them then secretly explained to me, "Please understand we have been sent here by somebody. You just get away for a moment, and we will ask for repayment directly from the man who called us here."

"I'll return myself what I owe! You had better all go away!"

My wish was immediately obeyed, and the people having left, I called Ch'it'ang into my presence and remonstrated with him. "Though a stupid elder brother, I have never committed any great wrongs. If you are thinking of my being made heir to uncle, remember that I did not receive a single cent of the family fortune. Do you suppose I came home to divide property with you instead of for the funeral? A man ought to stand on his own feet; I have come empty-handed, and empty-handed I go!" After saying this, I turned about and went behind the curtain again and cried bitterly by the coffin.

I then said good-bye to my mother and went to tell Ch'ingchün that I was going to a mountain to become a Taoist monk. While Ch'ingchün was just trying to persuade me not to do so, some friends of mine arrived. They were the brothers Hsia Nanhsün, literary name Tan-an, and Hsia Fengt'ai, literary name Yishan. They remonstrated with me in a very severe tone, and thus began:

　　"家庭若此，固堪动念；但足下父死而母尚存，妻丧而子未立，
乃竟飘然出世，于心安乎？"

　　余曰："然则如之何？"

　　淡安曰："奉屈暂居寒舍。闻石琢堂殿撰有告假回籍之信，盍俟
其归而往谒之？其必有以位置君也。"

　　余曰："凶丧未满百日，兄等有老亲在堂，恐多未便。"

　　揖山曰：愚兄弟之相邀，亦家君意也。足下如执以为不便，西邻
有禅寺，方丈僧与余交最善。足下设榻于寺中，何如？"余诺之。

　　青君曰："祖父所遗房产不下三四千金，既已分毫不取，岂自己
行囊亦舍去耶？我往取之，径送禅寺父亲处可也。"因是于行囊之外，
转得吾父所遗图书，砚台，笔筒数件。

"We don't blame you for being angry with this kind of a family, but although your father has died, your mother is still living, and although your wife is dead, your son is not independent yet. Have you really the heart to become a monk?"

"What am I going to do then?" I replied.

"For the time being," said Tan-an, "you could put up at our home. I hear that his honour Shih Chot'ang is coming home on leave from his office. Why don't you wait till he comes and see him about it? I am sure he will be able to give you a position."

"This is hardly proper," I said. "I am still in the hundred days of my mourning, and your parents are still living."

"Don't worry on that account," said Yishan. "for our father, too, joins us in the invitation. If you think it's not quite proper to do so, then there is a temple on the west of our home where the abbot is a good friend of mine. How about putting up there?" To this I agreed.

Then Ch'ingchün said to me, "Grandfather had left us a family property certainly not less than three or four thousand dollars. If you will not have a share of the property, will you not even take along your travelling bag? I'll fetch it myself and bring it to the temple for you." In this way not only did I get my travelling bag, but also found ingeniously stuck in it some books, paintings, ink slabs and pots for holding writing brushes left behind by my father.

　　寺僧安置予于大悲阁。阁南向,向东设神像。隔西首一间,设月窗,紧对佛龛,本为作佛事者斋食之地,余即设榻其中。临门有关圣提刀立像,极威武。院中有银杏一株,大三抱,荫覆满阁。夜静风声如吼。撝山常携酒果来对酌,曰:"足下一人独处,夜深不寐,得无畏怖耶?"

　　余曰:"仆一生坦直,胸无秽念,何怖之有?"

　　居未几,大雨倾盆,连宵达旦,三十余天。时虑银杏折枝,压梁倾屋,赖神默佑,竟得无恙。而外之墙坍屋倒者不可胜计,近处田禾俱被漂没。余则日与僧人作画,不见不闻。

The monk put me up at the Tower of Great Mercy. The tower faced south and on its east was a buddha. I occupied the western room which had a moon window exactly opposite the buddha, this being the room where pilgrims used to have their meals. At the door, there was a most imposing standing figure, representing General Kuan Yü, the Chinese God of War and Loyalty, holding a huge knife in his hand. A big maiden-hair tree stood in the yard, three fathoms in circumference, and cast a heavy shade over the whole tower. At night the wind would blow past the tree, making a roaring noise. Yishan often brought some wine and fruit to the place to have a drink between ourselves.

"Are you not afraid of staying here alone on a dark night?" he asked.

"No," I replied. "I have lived a straight life and have a free conscience, why should I be afraid?"

It happened that shortly after I moved in, there was a pouring rain which continued day and night for over a month. I was always afraid that some branch of the maiden-hair tree might break off and crash on to the roof, but, thanks to the protection of the gods, nothing happened. In the country around us, however, a great number of houses had fallen down and all the rice fields were flooded. I spent the days painting with the monk as if nothing had happened.

　　七月初，天始霁，揖山尊人号莼芗有交易赴崇明，偕余往，代笔书券得二十金。归，值吾父将安葬，启堂命逢森向余曰："叔因葬事乏用，欲助一二十金。"余拟倾囊与之。揖山不允，分帮其半。余即携青君先至墓所。

　　葬既毕，仍返大悲阁。九月杪，揖山有田在东海永泰沙，又偕余往收其息。盘桓两月，归已残冬，移寓其家雪鸿草堂度岁。真异姓骨肉也。

　　乙丑七月，琢堂始自都门回籍。琢堂名韫玉，字执如，琢堂其号也，与余为总角交。乾隆庚戌殿元，出为四川重庆守。白莲教之乱，三年戎马，极著劳绩。及归，相见甚欢。

At the beginning of the seventh moon, the sky cleared up and I went to the Ts'ungming Island as a personal secretary of Yishan's father, whose "fancy name" was Shünhsiang and who was going there on business. For this I received twenty dollars as remuneration. When I returned, they were making my father's grave and Ch'it'ang asked Fengsen to tell me that he was in need of money for the burial expenses and would I lend him ten or twenty dollars? I was going to turn over the money I had to him, but Yishan would not allow it and insisted on contributing half of the amount. I then went ahead to my father's grave, accompanied by Ch'ingchün.

After the burial, I returned to the Tower of Great Mercy. At the end of the ninth moon, Yishan had some rent to collect from his crops at Yungt'ai Beach in Tunghai and I accompanied him there, where we stayed for two months. When we returned, it was already late winter and I moved to his home at the Snow-and-Wild-Goose Study to pass the New Year. Yishan was, indeed, better to me than my own kin.

In the seventh moon of the year 1805, Chot'ang returned home from the capital. This was his "fancy name," while his real name was Yünyü and his literary name Chihju. He was a childhood chum of mine, took the first place in the imperial examinations in 1790 during the reign of Ch'ienlung, and then became magistrate of Chungking in Szechuen. During the rebellion of the White Lotus Secret Society, he won great merit for himself fighting the rebels for three years. When he returned, we were very glad to see each other.

　　旋于重九日，靑岩重赴四川重庆之任，邀余同往。余即叩别吾母于九妹倩陆尚吾家，盖先君故居已属他人矣。吾母嘱曰："汝弟不足恃，汝行须努力。重振家声，全望汝也。"逢森送余至半途，忽泪落不已，因嘱勿送而返。

　　舟出京口，琢堂有旧交王惕夫孝廉在淮扬盐署，绕道往晤，余与偕往，又得一顾芸娘之墓。返舟由长江溯流而上，一路游览名胜，至湖北之荆州，得升潼关观察之信，遂留余与其嗣君敦夫眷属等，暂寓荆州，琢堂轻骑减从至重庆度岁，遂由成都历栈道之任。丙寅二月，川眷始由水路往，至樊城登陆。途长费短，车重人多，毙马折轮，备尝辛苦。

On the Double Ninth Festival Day, he was going to his office at Chungking with his family and asked me to accompany him. I then said good-bye to my mother at the home of Loh Shangwu, the husband of my ninth sister, for by this time my father's home had already been sold. My mother gave me parting instructions as follows:"You should try your best to glorify the name of the family, for your younger brother will never amount to anything. Remember I depend entirely on you." Fengsen was seeing me off, but on the way he suddenly began to weep bitterly, and I bade him go home.

When our boat arrived at Kingk'ou [Chinkiang], Chot'ang said he wanted to see an old friend of his, Wang T'ifu, who was a *chüjen* and was working at the Salt Bureau in Yangchow. He was going out of his way to call on him and I accompanied him there, and thus had another chance to look at Yün's grave. Then we turned back and went up the Yangtze River and enjoyed all the scenery on the way. When we arrived at Kingchow, Hupeh, we learnt that my friend had been promoted a *taotai* at Tungkuan [in Honan]. He, therefore, asked me to stay at Kingchow with his son Tunfu and family, while he went to pass the New Year at Chungking with just a small entourage and went directly to his new office via Chengtu. In the second moon of the following year, his family at Szechuen then followed him there by boat up the river as far as Fanch'eng. From that point on, we had to travel by land. The way was very long and the expenses very heavy; with the heavy load of men and luggage, horses died and cartwheels were often broken on the road and it was altogether a tortuous journey.

　　抵潼关甫三月，琢堂又升山左廉访，清风两袖，眷属不能偕行，暂借潼川书院作寓。十月杪，始支山左廉俸，专人接眷；附有青君之书，骇悉逢森于四月间夭亡，始忆前之送余堕泪者，盖父子永诀也。呜呼！芸仅一子，不得延其嗣续耶！琢堂闻之，亦为之浩叹，赠余一妾，重入春梦。从此扰扰攘攘，又不知梦醒何时耳。

It was barely three months since his arrival at Tungkuan, when Chot'ang was again transferred to Shantung as inspector. As he was an upright official, having made no money from the people and therefore unable to pay the expenses to bring his family there, we remained temporarily at the T'ungch'uan College. Only at the end of the tenth moon did he receive his salary from his Shantung office, which enabled him to send for his family. In his letter he enclosed a note from Ch'ingchün, which informed me that Fengsen had died in the fourth moon. Then I began to understand that the tears he shed when sending me off from home were tears of farewell. Alas! Yün had only one son and must even he be taken away and not allowed to continue her line! Chot'ang was also greatly touched at the news, and presented me with a concubine. From that time on, I was again thrown into life's mad turmoil, a floating dream from which I do not know when I shall wake up!

Chapter Four

THE JOYS OF TRAVEL

卷四·浪游记快

　　余游幕三十年来，天下所未到者，蜀中，黔中与滇南耳。惜乎轮蹄征逐，处处随人；山水怡情，云烟过眼，不过领略其大概，不能探僻寻幽也。余凡事喜独出己见，不屑随人是非，即论诗品画，莫不存人珍我弃，人弃我取之意；故名胜所在，贵乎心得，有名胜而不觉其佳者，有非名胜而自以为妙者。聊以平生所历者记之。

For thirty years I worked as a government clerk in different yamen and practically visited every province except Szechuen, Kweichow and Yunnan. Unfortunately, I was not free to wander where I liked, inasmuch as I was always attached to some office, and could therefore only hastily enjoy such natural scenery as came my way, getting at most a general impression of things without the opportunity to explore the more unfrequented and out-of-the-way spots. I am by nature fond of forming my own opinions without regard to what others say. For instance, in the criticism of painting and poetry, I would value highly certain things that others look down upon, and think nothing of what others prize very highly. So it is also with natural scenery, whose true appreciation must come from one's own heart or not at all. There are famous scenic spots that do not at all appeal to me, and, on the other hand, certain places that are not at all famous but delighted me intensely. I will merely record here the places that I have visited.

　　余年十五时，吾父稼夫公馆于山阴赵明府幕中，有赵省斋先生名
传者，杭之宿儒也，赵明府延教其子，吾父命余亦拜投门下。暇日出
游，得至吼山，离城约十余里，不通陆路。近山见一石洞，上有片石，
横裂欲堕，即从其下荡舟入，豁然空其中，四面皆峭壁，俗名之曰水
园。临流建石阁五椽，对面石壁有"观鱼跃"三字。水深不测，相传
有巨鳞潜伏。余投饵试之，仅见不盈尺者出而唼食焉。阁后有道通旱
园，拳石乱叠，有横阔如掌者，有柱石平其顶而上加大石者，凿痕犹在，
一无可取。游览既毕，宴于水阁，命从者放爆竹，轰然一响，万山齐应，
如闻霹雳声。此幼时快游之始。惜乎兰亭、禹陵未能一到，至今以为憾。

When I was fifteen, my father Chiafu was working at the yamen at Shanyin with one official Chao, who employed a certain old scholar of Hangchow by the name of Chao Ch'üan, literary name Shengtsai, as private tutor for his son, and I was made by my father to study under him. Once I had the opportunity of visiting the Houshan Hill, which was over ten *li* from the city and could be reached only by a waterway. On approaching the hill, I saw there was a stone cave with a rock jutting out horizontally as if it was going to fall down. My boat passed under this and went inside the cave, commonly known as "Shuiyüan" (Water Park), which was very spacious within and surrounded on all sides by perpendicular rocks. There was a stone open tower overlooking the water, consisting of five beams, and a stone inscription on the opposite rock bearing the words, "Looking at Jumping Fish." The water was very deep at this spot and people said that there were some gigantic fish in it. I threw some crumbs down, but saw only small ones hardly a foot long come up to nibble them. A road led from the back of the open tower to "Hanyüan" (Land Park), where there was a jumble of rockery, standing in irregular profusion, some of them only as broad as the palm of a hand, and others being stone pillars with their tops ground even, and capped with huge rocks. The whole thing was artificial, the workman's marks being too apparent, and nothing good could be said for them. After going round the place, I had a picnic in the Water Park at the open tower by the waterside. I asked an attendant to fire some crackers, which made a noise like thunder, reverberating throughout the whole valley. This was my first taste of the joys of travel in my young days. Unfortunately I was not able to visit the Orchid Pavilion[1] and Emperor Yü's Tomb, a sin of omission which I very much regret to this day.

---

[1] Made famous by Wang Hsichih's essay. — *Tr.*

　　至山阴之明年，先生以亲老不远游，设帐于家。余遂从至杭，西湖之胜因得畅游。结构之妙，予以龙井为最，小有天园次之。石取天竺之飞来峰，城隍山之瑞石古洞。水取玉泉，以水清多鱼，有活泼趣也。大约至不堪者，葛岭之玛瑙寺。其余湖心亭，六一泉诸景，各有妙处，不能尽述；然皆不脱脂粉气，反不如小静室之幽僻，雅近天然。

　　苏小墓在西泠桥侧，土人指示，初仅半丘黄土而已。乾隆庚子，圣驾南巡，曾一询及。甲辰春，复举南巡盛典，则苏小墓已石筑其坟，作八角形，上立一碑，大书曰"钱塘苏小小之墓。"

The year following my arrival at Shanyin, my tutor asked me to study at his home, as he would not, on principle, leave his aged parents and stay far away from them. I then followed him to Hangchow and was thus enabled to see the scenic beauties of the famous West Lake. I regard Lungching (the Dragon Well) as the best in point of general plan and design, with the Hsiaoyüt'ien Garden (Little Paradise) coming next. For rocks I would prefer the Flying Peak of T'ienchu and the Ancient Cave of Precious Stones on the City God's Hill. For water, I prefer the Jade Spring, because its water is so clear and there are so many fish in it, giving an impression of natural life. Probably the worst is the Agate Temple of Kehling. There are, besides, beautiful places like the Mid-Lake Pavilion and the Six-One Spring, which it is impossible or unnecessary to describe in detail, being all suggestive of overdressed women with too much rouge and powder. There is a good and quiet secluded place like the Little Quiet Lodge, which has a natural beauty of its own, superior to them all.

The Tomb of Su Hsiaohsiao is situated by the side of the Hsiling Bridge. When the native people showed it to me, it was but a little mound of yellow earth. In the year 1780, when Emperor Ch'ienlung came down south, he once made a casual enquiry about it, and when he came again in the spring of 1784, the grave had already been reconstructed into a stone tomb of octagonal shape, with a stone tablet bearing the inscription: "The Tomb of Su Hsiaohsiao of Ch'ient'ang."

　　从此吊古骚人，不须徘徊探访矣！余思古来烈魄贞魂埋没不传者，固不可胜数，即传而不久者亦不为少；小小一名妓耳，自南齐至今，尽人而知之，此殆灵气所钟，为湖山点缀耶？

　　桥北数武有崇文书院，余曾与同学赵缉之投考其中。时值长夏，起极早，出钱塘门，过昭庆寺，上断桥，坐石阑上。旭日将升，朝霞映于柳外，尽态极妍。白莲香里，清风徐来，令人心骨皆清。步至书院，题犹未出也。午后交卷。偕缉之纳凉于紫云洞，大可容数十人，石窍上透日光。有人设短几矮凳，卖酒于此。解衣小酌，尝鹿脯甚妙，佐以鲜菱雪藕，微酣出洞。

Since then, poets who come to visit the ancient beauty's tomb have not to hunt round for it. Any number of virtuous and high-principled women have lived and died whose names were never handed down to posterity, and many others who were remembered for a short period and then forgotten, but here was Su Hsiaohsiao, merely a famous courtesan, who has been remembered by everybody from the South Ch'i Dynasty down to the present. Was this perhaps due to the fact that she was made of the spirit of nature's hills and dales and was in this way destined to grace the beauties of the Lake?

A few paces north from the Hsiling Bridge there was the Ts'ungwen College, where I used to take the examinations together with a fellow class-mate Chao Ch'ichih. It was summer then and we would get up very early, pass the Ch'ient'ang Gate and the Chaoch'ing Temple, come down the Broken Bridge and sit down on its stone balustrade. The sun was rising then and there was a stretch of morning haze behind the rows of willow-trees, giving a most charming effect. The air was filled with the fragrance of the lotus flowers and a gentle breeze would blow by, making one feel light of heart and body. By the time we reached the College on foot, the subjects for the examinations were not yet given out. We handed in our papers in the afternoon, and went to cool ourselves at the Purple Clouds Cave. The cave was big enough to hold several dozen people, and there was a fissure among the rocks on its roof admitting a ray of sunlight. A wine-seller had provided a low table and some stools at this place. We then took off our long gowns and had a little drink; the shredded deermeat was very delicious and we took it with fresh lotus roots and water caltrops, leaving the cave slightly drunk.

　　缉之曰："上有朝阳台，颇高旷，盍往一游？"余亦兴发，奋勇登其巅，觉西湖如镜，杭城如丸，钱塘江如带，极目可数百里，此生平第一大观也。坐良久，阳乌将落，相携下山，南屏晚钟动矣。韬光、云栖路远未到。其红门局之梅花，姑姑庙之铁树，不过尔尔。紫阳洞予以为必可观，而访寻得之，洞口仅容一指，涓涓流水而已。相传中有洞天，恨不能抉门而入。

　　清明日，先生春祭扫墓，挈余同游。墓在东岳。是乡多竹，坟丁掘未出土之毛笋，形如梨而尖，作羹供客。余甘之，尽其两碗。

Ch'ichih proposed that we should go up to the Morning Glory Terrace, which commanded a high and open view of the country. Being in a mood for adventure, we climbed up to its very top where, as we looked down, the West Lake appeared like a mirror and the City of Hangchow like a tiny little mud-cake, while the Ch'ient'ang River wended its way like an encircling girdle. We could see at least hundreds of *li* away; in fact, this was the grandest sight I ever saw in my life. After sitting on top there for quite a while, the sun was going down and we came down the hill, when the sound of the temple bells from the South-Screen Hill reached our ears. We did not visit Taokuang and Yünsi because they were too far away. The plum-blossoms of the Red Gate Ground and the ironwood trees of the Kuku Temple were, in fact, not much to look at. The Purple Sun Cave, which we had thought worth seeing and took some trouble to reach, proved to be merely a spring with water flowing down from a hole, the "entrance to the cave," which was but the size of a finger. Tradition says that there was a big cave inside and I regretted very much not to be able to break into it.

On the *Ch'ingming* Festival,[1] my tutor was going to visit his ancestral grave and brought me along. The grave was situated at Tungyo, or East Sacred Hill. The country was full of bamboos and the care-taker of the place entertained us with soup of bamboo-shoots, which were dug up before they grew above the ground, and looked like pears, only a little more pointed. It was so delicious that I drank two bowls of it.

[1] A festival which falls on any unfixed date somewhere round the middle part of the spring months. On this day people are accustomed to pay their visits to their ancestral tombs in the country.

　　先生曰："噫！是虽味美而克心血，宜多食肉以解之。"余素不贪屠门之嚼，至是饭量且因笋而减。归途觉烦躁，唇舌几裂。过石屋洞，不甚可观。水乐洞峭壁多藤萝，入洞如斗室，有泉流甚急，其声琅琅。池广仅三尺，深五寸许，不溢亦不竭。余俯流就饮，烦躁顿解。洞外二小亭，坐其中，可听泉声。衲子请观万年缸。缸在香积厨，形甚巨，以竹引泉灌其内，听其满溢。年久结苔厚尺许；冬日不冰，故不损也。

"You'd better look out," said my tutor. "Bamboo-shoots have an action on the heart-beat, although they are so delicious. You must take a lot of meat together with them." I was not usually fond of meat, and this time I ate so much bamboo-shoots that I could scarcely take any rice. On my way home, I found my throat parched and my tongue and lips all dried up. We passed the Stone House Cave which was not much to look at. Another cave, the Cave of Aquatic Pleasure, was full of steep rocks covered with ivy. I entered the cave, which was small like an attic, and saw a gurgling spring, which collected at a pool about three feet wide and five inches deep only; the water, I was told, remained at that constant level throughout the year. I knelt down on the ground to drink from the pool and felt an immense relief in my throat. There were two little pavilions outside the cave where one could sit and listen to the murmuring spring. A monk came along and asked us to see the "Jar of Ten Thousand Years"; this was a big jar in the kitchen, with spring water running into it through a bamboo pole and thus always kept full to over-flowing. As that jar had lain there for years and years, it was covered with moss over a foot long, and as the temperature never went below zero, the jar was never broken.

　　辛丑秋八月，吾父病疟返里。寒索火，热索冰，余谏不听，竟转伤寒，病势日重。余侍奉汤药，昼夜不交睫者几一月。吾妇芸娘亦大病，恹恹在床。心境恶劣，莫可名状。吾父呼余嘱之曰："我病恐不起。汝守数本书，终非糊口计。我托汝于盟弟蒋思斋，仍继吾业可耳。"越日思斋来，即于榻前命拜为师。未几，得名医徐观莲先生诊治，父病渐痊；芸亦得徐力起床。而余则从此习幕矣。此非快事，何记于此？曰：此抛书浪游之始，故记之。

In the eighth moon of 1781, my father returned home, laid up with malaria. He would ask for fire when in a cold spell and ask for ice when in high fever, despite my repeated advice to the contrary, and in this way, it turned into typhoid, which grew from bad to worse every day. I attended on him day and night and never slept a wink for almost a month. My wife, Yünniang, also fell seriously ill at this time and was confined to bed; everything was in a muddle and I felt very miserable. "I am afraid I shall never get well," said my father to me one day, calling me to his bedside for final instructions. "I don't think you can make a living with the knowledge derived from a few books, and I am going to place you in charge of a sworn brother of mine, Chiang Ssŭtsai, who will bring you up to follow my profession." Ssŭtsai turned up next day and I was made to kowtow to him as pupil to tutor by my father's bedside. Soon afterwards, however, my father was attended to by a famous doctor, Mr. Hsü Kuanlien, and gradually got well; Yün, too, was cured by the same doctor and was able to leave her bed. Thus I began my training as a yamen clerk. I mention this unpleasant episode here in my record of the joys of travel because, through this change of profession, I was enabled to leave my studies and travel a great deal.

　　思斋先生名襄。是年冬，即相随习幕于奉贤官舍。有同习幕者，顾姓名金鉴，字鸿干，号紫霞，亦苏州人也，为人慷慨刚毅，直谅不阿，长余一岁，呼之为兄，鸿干即毅然呼余为弟，倾心相交。此余第一知交也，惜以二十二岁卒。余即落落寡交。今年且四十有六矣，茫茫沧海，不知此生再遇知己如鸿干者否？忆与鸿干订交，襟怀高旷，时兴山居之想。

　　重九日，余与鸿干俱在苏。有前辈王小侠与吾父稼夫公唤女伶演剧，宴客吾家。余患其扰，先一日约鸿干赴寒山登高，藉访他日结庐之地。芸为整理小酒榼。

My teacher's name was Hsiang. I followed him in the winter of that year to the yamen of Fenghsien. There was a colleague of mine, also learning the same profession at the place; his name was Ku Chinchien, literary name Hungkan and "fancy name" Purple Haze. Ku was also a native of Soochow and was by nature a big-hearted, frank and straightforward fellow. As he was a year older, I called him "elder brother," and he called me "younger brother" and we became fast friends. Hungkan was in fact the best friend I had in this world. Unfortunately he died at twenty-two, and now in my forty-sixth year I doubt if I could find another friend like him in this wide, wide world. I remember that when we began our friendship, our minds were full of noble thoughts and we often thought of living a quiet life in the mountains.

On the Double Ninth Festival, it happened that we were both at Soochow. That day we were having some theatrical performances at home by some actresses called there by my father and his friend Wang Hsiaohsia. Knowing of this beforehand, and disliking the noise and confusion, I had arranged with Hungkan to go to the Hanshan Temple that day and climb high mountains [as was customary on this festival], incidentally looking for a place for retirement. Yün had prepared a small picnic case of wine and eatables for us.

　　越日天将晓，鸿干已登门相邀，遂携榼出胥门，入面肆，各饱食。渡胥江，步至横塘枣市桥，雇一叶扁舟，到山日犹未午。舟子颇循良，令其粜米煮饭。余两人上岸，先至中峰寺。寺在支硎古刹之南，循道而上。寺藏深树，山门寂静，地僻僧闲，见余两人不衫不履，不甚接待。余等志不在此，未深入。归舟，饭已熟。

　　饭毕，舟子携榼相随，嘱其子守船。由寒山至高义园之白云精舍。轩临峭壁，下凿小池，围以石树，一泓秋水。崖悬薜荔，墙积莓苔。坐轩下，惟闻落叶萧萧，悄无人迹。出门有一亭，嘱舟子坐此相候。余两人从石罅中入，名"一线天"，循级盘旋，直造其巅，曰"上白云"。有庵已坍颓，存一危栈，仅可远眺。小憩片刻，即相扶而下。

At dawn, Hungkan appeared at my home, and we brought the case along, passed the Hsümen Gate, and went into a noodle shop to have our breakfast. Then we crossed the Hsükiang River and walked by foot to the Date-Market Bridge at Hengt'ang. From there we engaged a boat, reaching the place shortly before noon. The boatman was an honest sort and we asked him to buy some rice and prepare lunch for us, while we went ashore and visited first the Central Peak Temple, which stood to the south of Chih-hsing Ancient Temple. Following the path up, we saw that the Central Peak Temple was hidden away in a thick wood. The place was secluded, and the monks had nothing to do, but seeing our appearance, for we were not properly dressed as yamen clerks should be, gave us a very cold welcome. As we did not intend to see this place in particular, we did not go in. By the time we returned to the boat, the lunch was ready.

After lunch, the boatman followed us with the picnic case, leaving his son to look after the boat. We then went on from the Hanshan Temple to the White Cloud Villa, by the Garden of High Virtue. This Villa was situated at the foot of a cliff with a little pond below, surrounded by rockery and trees. The cliff was overgrown with *Ficus pumila* and the walls were covered with moss. We sat in the hall, listening to the silent swish of falling leaves, with not a soul in sight. There was a pavilion outside where we bade the boatman wait for us, while we two went through a fissure in the rock, called "A Ray from the Sky," and following the narrow winding steps up, we reached the top which was called the "Upper White Clouds." There was a dilapidated temple there with a solitary tower still standing, useful now only for obtaining a good view of the surrounding country. After resting there for a while, we helped each other down.

舟子曰:"登高忘携酒榼矣。"

鸿干曰:"我等之游,欲觅偕隐地耳,非专为登高也。"

舟子曰:"离此南行二三里,有上沙村,多人家,有隙地。我有表戚范姓居是村,盍往一游?"

余喜曰:"此明末徐俟斋先生隐居处也。有园闻极幽雅,从未一游。"

于是舟子导往。村在两山夹道中。园依山而无石,老树多极纡回盘郁之势。亭榭窗栏尽从朴素,竹篱茆舍,不愧隐者之居。中有皂荚亭,树大可两抱。余所历园亭,此为第一。

"You've just 'climbed to a high place' and forgot to bring along your picnic case!" remarked the boatman.

"We came here," replied Hungkan, "not merely to climb to high places, but to look round for a place of retirement."

"As for that," said the boatman, "there is a village to the south about two or three *li* from here, called Shangsha, with many inhabitants, and there are some vacant lots in it. I have a relative, one Mr. Fan, staying at this village; why not go and take a look?"

"This is the place of retirement of Mr. Hsü Ssŭtsai at the end of the Ming Dynasty," I said, delighted at the suggestion. "I hear there is a very nice and secluded garden which I have not seen yet."

We then followed the boatman as our guide. The village stood on a path between two hills. The garden was situated on a hillside but devoid of all rocks; on the other hand, there were many old trees with winding branches of great strength and beauty. The pavilions, water-sheds, windows and railings were designed in a very simple style and there were bamboo fences and hay-thatched mud cottages, as was becoming the residence of a recluse. In the centre there was a pavilion with a honey-locust tree about two fathoms in circumference nearby. Of all the gardens I have seen, I consider this the best.

　　园左有山，俗呼鸡笼山，山峰直竖，上加大石，如杭城之瑞石古洞，而不及其玲珑。旁一青石如榻，鸿干卧其上曰："此处仰观峰岭，俯视园亭，既旷且幽，可以开樽矣。"因拉舟子同饮，或歌或啸，大畅胸怀。土人知余等觅地而来，误以为堪舆，以某处有好风水相告。鸿干曰："但期合意，不论风水。"（岂意竟成谶语！）

　　酒瓶既罄，各采野菊插满两鬓。归舟，日已将没，更许抵家，客犹未散。芸私告余曰："女伶中有兰官者，端庄可取。"余假传母命呼之入内，握其腕而睨之，果丰颐白腻。

On the left of the garden there was a hill, commonly known as the Chicken Coop Hill, whose peak went up perpendicularly, with rocks at the top resembling those at the Ancient Cave of Precious Stones at Hangchow, but not perforated in the same manner, or quite as elegant as the latter. Hungkan sought out a bed of green stone where he lay down and exclaimed, "Now here I can look up at the mountain peaks above and look down upon the garden and pavilions below. It's as airy here as it is secluded—let's have our wine now!" Then we asked the boatman to drink with us, and sang or whistled to our hearts' content. The peasants of this place learnt that we were looking for a lot, and, thinking that we were trying to find a propitious place for burial, came and told us about a good spot. "We don't care where we are buried," said Hungkan. "Any place that is to our liking will do!" Who would know that this proved to be an ill omen!

When the wine-pot was all empty, we went about picking lilies of the valley to decorate the temples of our queues with. By the time we reached our boat, the sun was already going down, and when we arrived home about nine o'clock in the evening the guests had not yet dispersed. Yün secretly said to me, "There is an actress called Lankuan who is charming and dignified and of the right type." I called her in, pretending that my mother wanted to see her. Holding her wrist and surveying her carefully, I saw that she was indeed full and white and soft.

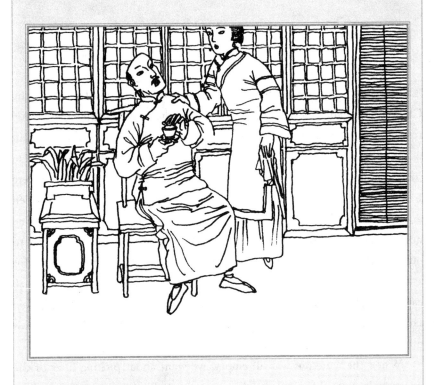

余顾芸曰:"美则美矣,终嫌名不称实。"

芸曰:"肥者有福相。"

余曰:"马嵬之祸,玉环之福安在?"

芸以他辞遣之出,谓余曰:"今日君又大醉耶?"余乃历述所游,芸亦神往者久之。

癸卯春,余从思斋先生就维扬之聘,始见金、焦面目。金山宜远观,焦山宜近视。惜余往来其间,未尝登眺。渡江而北,渔洋所谓"绿杨城郭是扬州"一语,已活现矣。平山堂离城约三四里,行其途有八九里。虽全是人功,而奇思幻想,点缀天然;即阆苑瑶池,琼楼玉宇,谅不过此。其妙处在十余家之园亭,合而为一,联络至山,气势俱贯。

Turning to Yün, I said, "She is quite beautiful, but her name ('Orchid') doesn't agree with her figure."

"But a plump person has good luck," replied Yün.

"What about the fat Yang Kueifei who died at Mawei?"

After sending her away on some pretext, Yün said to me, "Were you happily drunk again today?" Then I told her all that we had seen on the way and she listened to it in transport for a long time.

In the spring of 1783, I accompanied my teacher to Yangchow and in this way got a glimpse of the Chinshan and Chiaoshan Hills [at Chinkiang]. The former should be looked at from a distance, and the latter at close range; unfortunately I failed to visit these hills, although I passed them many times. On crossing the Yangtze River to the north, I saw before my very eyes the "walls of green willows" of Yangchow, as the poet Wang Yüyang described it. The P'ingshan Hall was about three or four *li* from the city, but was reached by a winding route of eight or nine *li*. Although this entire landscape was built by human labour, it was so ingeniously planned that it looked like a bit of nature, suggesting to me the "marble halls" and "emerald pools" and phantom gardens of Fairyland itself. The beauty of the place consisted in the fact that over a dozen private villas and home gardens combined to form a huge park, stretching all the way from the city to the hill, with a unity all its own.

　　其最难位置处，出城入景，有一里许紧沿城郭。夫城缀于旷远重山间，方可入画。园林有此，蠢笨绝伦。而观其或亭或台，或墙或石，或竹或树，半隐半露间，使游人不觉其触目；此非胸有丘壑者断难下手。

　　城尽以虹园为首折而向北，有石梁曰"虹桥"。不知园以桥名乎？桥以园名乎？荡舟过，曰"长堤春柳"。此景不缀城脚而缀于此，更见布置之妙。再折而西，垒土立庙，曰"小金山"。有此一挡，便觉气势紧凑，亦非俗笔。

From the point of view of landscape designing, the most difficult part to lay out satisfactorily was a space of over a *li* that lay close by the city wall. A city should, in order to be picturesque, be built against a background of a vast countryside with ranges of hills in the distance; it was, therefore, a most difficult problem to have pavilions and parks around it without achieving a stupid, closed-in effect. But the whole thing was so contrived, with a pavilion here and a terrace there, and glimpses of walls and rocks and trees and bamboo groves so cleverly designed that there was not the slightest bit of obtrusiveness to the tourist's eye. Only a master architect of the mind could have conceived and executed this.

The stretch began with the Rainbow Garden immediately adjoining the city wall, and after a turn to the north, came the Rainbow Bridge: I do not know whether the garden took its name from the bridge or the bridge from the garden. Rowing past these places, one came to the scene called "Spring Willows on a Long Embankment." It was a striking proof of the ingenuity of the designer, that this scene was placed at this spot and not immediately close to the city wall. With another turn to the west, there was an artificial mound with a temple on it, called "The Little Chinshan."[1] This was also a master stroke, for with this hill blocking the view, the picture became tightened and wonderfully compact.

[1] Or Little Gold Hill, after the Chinshan of Chinkiang. — *Tr.*

闻此地本沙土，屡筑不成，用木排若干，层叠加土，费数万金乃成。若非商家，乌能如是。

过此有胜概楼，年年观竞渡于此，河面较宽。南北跨一莲花桥。桥门通八面，桥面设五亭，扬人呼为"四盘一暖锅"。此思穷力竭之为，不甚可取。桥南有莲心寺。寺中突起喇嘛白塔，金顶缨络，高矗云霄，殿角红墙，松柏掩映，钟磬时闻；此天下园亭所未有者。

I was told that owing to the fact that the soil here consisted mainly of sand, they had tried several times to build the mound without success, until wooden piles had to be sunk into the ground at successive heights and then earth piled on to them, the whole work thus costing several tens of thousands of dollars. No one except the rich salt merchants [of Yangchow] could have carried through a project like this.

After this we came to the Tower of Triumphal Delight, where the waterway became broader and people used to hold annual boat races on the Dragon Boat Festival. This was spanned over by the Lotus Bridge running north and south. The bridge was situated on a central point, and on its top were five pavilions, with four at the corners and one at the centre, called by the natives of Yangchow "Four Dishes and One Soup." I did not like it because the design was too laborious or suggested too much mental effort. On the south of the bridge there was the Lotus-Seed Temple, with a Tibetan pagoda rising straight up from its midst and its golden dome rising into the clouds; with the terra-cotta walls and temple roofs nestling under the kind shade of pine-trees and cypresses and the sounds of temple bells and *ch'ing* [musical stone] coming to the traveller's ears intermittently—all combining to achieve a unique effect that could not be duplicated in any other pleasure garden of the world.

　　过桥见三层高阁，画栋飞檐，五采绚烂，叠以太湖石，围以白石阑，名曰"五云多处"；如作文中间之大结构也。过此名"蜀冈朝旭，"平坦无奇，且属附会。将及山，河面渐束，堆土植竹树，作四五曲；似已山穷水尽，而忽豁然开朗，平山之万松林已列于前矣。"平山堂"为欧阳文忠公所书。所谓淮东第五泉，真者在假山石洞中，不过一井耳，味与天泉同；其荷亭中之六孔铁井栏者，乃系假设，水不堪饮。九峰园另在南门幽静处，别饶天趣，余以为诸园之冠。康山未到，不识如何。

After passing by the bridge, I saw a high three-storeyed tower with projecting eaves and painted girders in rainbow hues, decorated with rocks from the Taihu Lake and surrounded by white marble balustrades. This place was called "Where the Five-colored Clouds Are Abundant," its position in this picture suggesting the main turning-point of a literary composition. After this we came to a place known as "Morning Sun on the Szechuen Hill"—rather commonplace and uninteresting to me besides being artificial. As we were approaching the hill, the waterway narrowed down and lost itself in four or five bends formed by blocking the water's path with earth piled on the banks and planting them with bamboos and trees.

It was then as if the spirit of the place had spent itself when, all of a sudden, a beautiful view opened up before my eyes with the "Forest of Ten Thousand Pines" of the P'ingshan Hall before me. The three characters "P'ingshant'ang" were written by Ouyang Hsiu himself.[1] The genuine spring, called the "Fifth Best Spring, East of Huai River" was situated in a grotto, being nothing but a well whose water tasted like that of natural mountain springs, this being usually confused with the other well at the Lotus Pavilion with an iron cover on top bearing six holes, whose water was flat and tasteless. The Garden of Nine Peaks was situated in another secluded spot outside the South Gate; it had a natural charm of its own and in my opinion should be regarded as the best of all the gardens round the place. I did not go to the K'angshan Hill and have no idea what it is like.

[1] This was where the Sung scholar stayed and has now been made a temple to his honour. — *Tr.*

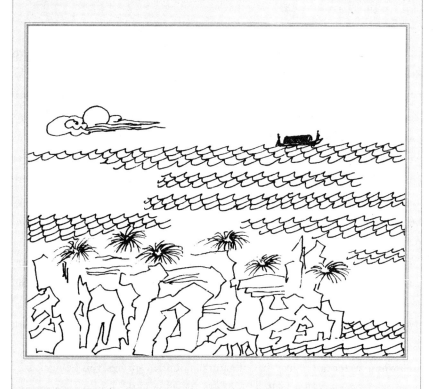

　　此皆言其大概。其工巧处，精美处，不能尽述。大约宜以艳妆美人目之，不可作浣纱溪上观也。余适恭逢南巡盛典，各工告竣，敬演接驾点缀，因得畅其大观，亦人生难遇者也。

　　甲辰之春，余随侍吾父于吴江何明府幕中，与山阴章苹江，武林章映牧，苕溪顾霭泉诸公同事，恭办南斗圩行宫，得第二次瞻仰天颜。一日，天将晚矣，忽动归兴。有办差小快船，双橹两桨，于太湖飞棹疾驰，吴俗呼为"出水缲头"，转瞬已至吴门桥；即跨鹤腾空，无此神爽。抵家，晚餐未熟也。

The above is merely a rough sketch of the place, with no attempt to go into its artistic beauties and details of workmanship. In general, I would say, the place looked more like a beautiful woman in a gorgeous costume than a pretty country maid washing on a river bank. It happened that I visited the place shortly after it had been done up expressly for the visit of Emperor Ch'ienlung, and thus saw it at its best—an opportunity which rarely comes to a person in a life-time.

In the spring of 1784, I accompanied my father to the yamen of Wukiang under the magistrate Mr. Ho, where I had colleagues like Chang Pinchiang of Shanyin, Chang Yingmu of Wulin and Ku Aich'üan of T'iaoch'i. There we had the privilege of preparing a provisional palace for Emperor at Nantouyü, and thus had the honour of seeing His Majesty a second time. One day [during this occasion], I suddenly thought of returning home when it was already approaching sundown. I got a small "fast boat," which was the kind used for fast official errands with two oars at the sides and two *yaolu* at the stern. This kind was called in Soochow "Horse's Head on the Surf" because it went so fast on the Taihu water. Quick as riding upon a stork in the air, I reached the Wumen Bridge in a second, and reached home before supper was ready.

　　吾乡素尚繁华，至此日之争奇夺胜，较昔尤奢。灯彩眩眸，笙歌聒耳，古人所谓"画栋雕甍"，"珠帘绣幕"，"玉阑干"，"锦步障"，不啻过之。余为友人东拉西扯，助其插花结彩。闲则呼朋引类，剧饮狂歌，畅怀游览。少年豪兴，不倦不疲。苟生于盛世而仍居僻壤，安得此游观哉！

　　是年，何明府因事被议，吾父即就海宁王明府之聘。嘉兴有刘蕙阶者，长斋侫佛，来拜吾父。其家在烟雨楼侧，一阁临河，曰水月居，其诵经处也，洁净如僧舍。烟雨楼在镜湖之中，四岸皆绿杨，惜无多竹。有平台可远眺。渔舟星列，漠漠平波，似宜月夜。衲子备素斋甚佳。

The people of my district were usually given to luxuries, and on this day they were still more extravagant. I saw dazzling lanterns and heard music of the flute and song all over the place, suggesting to me the "painted beams and carved girders," "beaded curtains and embroidered screens," "jade railings," and "screens of [women in] embroidered shoes" mentioned in ancient litearture. I was dragged about by my friends to help them in arranging flowers and hanging silk sashes. In our spare time, we would get together and indulge ourselves in wine and song or go about the place. Like all young people, we went through all this din and commotion without feeling tired. I would not have seen all this, if I had been living in an out-of-the-way village, even though it was a time of national peace and order.

That year Ho, the magistrate, was dismissed for some reason or other, and my father went to work with another magistrate Wang at Haining [in Chekiang]. There was a Mr. Liu Hueichieh of Kashing, a devoted buddhist, who came to call on my father. His home was situated by the side of the Tower of Mist and Rain [at Kashing], and had an open tower called Moon-in-the-Water Lodge overlooking the river. This was where he used to recite buddhist books, and was arranged spick and span like a monk's studio. The Tower of Mist and Rain was in the middle of the Mirror Lake, and had an open terrace looking out on green willows on the banks all around; had there been more bamboos, the view would have been perfect. Fishing boats lay about on the stretch of calm water—a scene which seemed to be best looked at under the moonlight. The monks there could prepare very excellent vegetarian food.

　　至海宁，与白门史心月，山阴俞午桥同事。心月一子名烛衡，澄静缄默，彬彬儒雅，与余莫逆；此生平第二知心交也，惜萍水相逢，聚首无多日耳。游陈氏安澜园，地占百亩，重楼复阁，夹道回廊。池甚广，桥作六曲形，石满藤萝，凿痕全掩；古木千章，皆有参天之势，鸟啼花落，如入深山。此人工而归于天然者，余所历平地之假石园亭，此为第一。曾于桂花楼中张宴，诸味尽为花气所夺，惟酱姜味不变。姜桂之性老而愈辣，以喻忠节之臣，洵不虚也。

At Haining I was working with Shih Hsinyüeh of Pomen [Nanking] and Yü Wuch'iao of Shanyin as my colleagues. Hsinyüeh had a son called Choheng, who was gentle and quiet of disposition, being the second best friend I had in life. Unfortunately, we met only for a short time and then parted like duckweed on the water. I also visited the "Garden of Peaceful Eddies" of Mr. Ch'en, which occupied over a hundred *mow* and had any number of towers, buildings, terraces and winding corridors. There was a wide pond with a zigzag bridge of six bends across it; the rocks were covered with ivy and creepers which helped to make them look so much heads to the sky, and in the midst of singing more natural; a thousand old trees reared their birds and falling petals, I felt like transported into a deep mountain forest. Of all the gardens I had seen built with artificial rockeries and pavilions on a flat ground, this was the one which approached nature most. One day we had a dinner at the Cassia Tower and the flavours of the food were simply lost in the fragrance of the flowers around— with the exception of pickled ginger, which remained sharp and pungent. The ginger is by its nature the more biting the older it becomes, and it seems to me extremely appropriate therefore for it to be compared to old dour, veteran ministers of state, who often have more guts than the young ones.

　　出南门，即大海。一日两潮，如万丈银堤破海而过。船有迎潮者，
潮至，反棹相向。于船头设一木招，状如长柄大刀。招一捺，潮即分破，
船即随招而入。俄顷始浮起，拨转船头，随潮而去，顷刻百里。

　　塘上有塔院，中秋夜曾随吾父观潮于此。循塘东约三十里，名尖
山，一峰突起，扑入海中。山顶有阁，匾曰"海阔天空，"一望无际，
但见怒涛接天而已。

　　余年二十有五，应徽州绩溪克明府之招。由武林下"江山船，"
过富春山，登子陵钓台。台在山腰，一峰突起，离水十余丈。

Going out of the South Gate, one came upon the great sea, its white-crested bores rushing by twice daily with the ebb and tide like mileslong silvery embankments. There were surfriding boats lying in wait with the bow facing the on-coming bore. At the bow of the boat was placed a wooden board shaped like a big knife for cutting the water when the bore came. With a movement of the cutter, the tide was divided and the boat took a dive into the water. After a while it came up again, and turning round, it followed the surf up the bay for miles with a tremendous speed.

On the embankment, there was a pagoda in an enclosure where I once viewed the bore on the night of a Mid-Autumn Festival [the fifteenth of the eighth moon] with my father. About thirty *li* eastwards further down the embankment, there was the Needle Hill, which rose up abruptly and ended up in the sea. A tower on its top bore the signboard: "The Sea is Wide and the Sky Spacious," from which place one could gain an unlimited view of the universe, with nothing except angry sea waves rising to meet the sky at the horizon.

I received an invitation to go to Chich'i in Hweichow [in Anhwei] from the magistrate Mr. K'eh there, when I was twenty-five years of age. I took a river junk from Hangchow, sailed up the Fuch'un River and visited the Fishing Terrace of Yen Tzuling. This so-called "Fishing Terrace" was located halfway up the Fuch'un Hill in the form of an overhanging cliff over a hundred feet above the water level.

　　岂汉时之水竟与峰齐耶？月夜泊界口，有巡检署。"山高月小，水落石出"，此景宛然。黄山仅见其脚，惜未一瞻面目。

　　绩溪城处于万山之中，弹丸小邑，民情淳朴。近城有石镜山。由山弯中曲折一里许，悬崖急湍，湿翠欲滴；渐高，至山腰，有一方石亭，四面皆陡壁。亭左石削如屏，青色光润，可鉴人形。俗传能照前生；黄巢至此，照为猿猴形，纵火焚之，故不复现。

Could it be that it was on the same level with the river in the Han Dynasty? On a moon-lit night, our boat anchored at Chiehk'ou, where there was an inspector's office. The moon seemed so small on the top of the high mountain and rocks stood up above the surface of the water, making a most enchanting picture. I also got a glimpse of the foot of Huangshan, or the Yellow Mountains, but unfortunately could not go up and explore the whole place.

The town of Chich'i is a very small one, being situated in a mountainous region and inhabited by a people of very simple ways. There is a hill near the town called the Stone Mirror Hill. One goes up by a zigzag mountain path for over a *li*, after which one sees jagged rocks and flying waterfalls, with the place so moist and green that it seems literally to ooze a kind of verdant radiance. Going higher half-way up the hillside, one sees a square stone pavilion, with perpendicular rocks on all sides as its walls. The sides of the pavilion are as straight as screen and of a green colour, being brilliant enough to reflect one's image. Local tradition has it that this mirror could reflect one's previous existence and that when Huangch'ao[1] arrived here, he saw in it his own image in the shape of a monkey and was so infuriated that he set fire to it; so from that time on, the Stone Mirror has lost its occult properties.

[1] The great bandit chief at the end of the Han Dynasty. — *Tr.*

　　离城十里有火云洞天，石纹盘结，凹凸巉岩，如黄鹤山樵笔意，而杂乱无章。洞石皆深绛色。旁有一庵甚幽静。盐商程虚谷曾招游，设宴于此。席中有肉馒头，小沙弥眈眈旁视，授以四枚。临行以番银二圆为酬。山僧不识，推不受。告以一枚可易青钱七百余文。僧以近无易处，仍不受。乃攒凑青蚨六百文付之，始欣然作谢。他日，余邀同人携榼再往。老僧嘱曰："曩者小徒不知食何物而腹泻，今勿再与。"可知藜藿之腹不受肉味，良可叹也。

Ten *li* from the town, there was the Cave of Burning Clouds, with rocks in twisted, jagged and most irregular formations, like the rock paintings of the "Woodcutter of Yellow Stork Hill,"[1] but the whole thing was in a sort of jumble without any plan or purpose. The rocks of the cave were of a deep red colour, with a very nice and quiet temple by its side. Once I was invited to dine there by a salt merchant called Ch'eng Hsüku. We were eating some *mant'ou*[2] with stuffing of mince-meat and an acolyte was watching us eating with wide open eyes, which induced me to give him four pieces. As we were leaving, we gave the old monk two Mexican dollars as tips, but the monk did not know what they were and would not accept them. I told him that one such dollar could be exchanged for over seven hundred cash, but the monk still declined to accept them on the ground that he could not exchange them in the neighbourhood. Then we got together six hundred cash and gave them to the monk, which he gladly received. It happened that I went there some days later with some of my friends, bringing along a basket of eatables. The old monk told me that the acolyte had developed diarrhoea after we had left there the last time, that he did not know what we had given him to eat and that we should refrain from doing any such thing again. It seemed then unfortunately true that a vegetarian stomach cannot hold non-vegetarian food.

[1] Pen name of a Yüan painter, Wang Meng. — *Tr.*
[2] Chinese bun. — *Tr.*

　　余谓同人曰："作和尚者必居此等僻地，终身不见不闻，或可修真养静。若吾乡之虎丘山，终日目所见者妖童艳妓，耳所听者弦索笙歌，鼻所闻者佳肴美酒，安得身如枯木，心如死灰哉！"

　　又去城三十里，名曰仁里，有花果会，十二年一举，每举各出盆花为赛。余在绩溪适逢其会，欣然欲往，苦无轿马，乃教以断竹为杠，缚椅为轿，雇人肩之而去。同游者惟同事许策廷，见者无不哧笑。至其地，有庙，不知供何神。庙前旷处高搭戏台，画梁方柱，极其巍焕，近视则纸扎彩画，抹以油漆者。

And I said to my friends, "It seems that a monk ought to stay in a secluded place like this, completely shut out from the world, in order to achieve true peace of mind. The monks at Huch'iu Hill, at my native place [Soochow], for instance, see nothing except handsome boys and pretty sing-song girls all day. They hear nothing but string instruments and the flute and singing, and smell nothing but excellent wine and delicious dishes. How could they forget the life of the senses and live like dried-up logs and dead ashes?"

There was a village, called the Benevolence Village, thirty *li* from the town, where they had a festival of flowers and fruit-trees every twelve years, during which a flower show was held. I was lucky enough to be there at the time and gladly undertook the journey to the place. There being no sedan-chairs or horses for hire, I taught the people to make some bamboos into carrying poles, and tie a chair on them, which served as a makeshift. There was only another colleague going along with me, one Hsü Ch'eht'ing, and all the people who saw us carried on the conveyance were greatly amused. When we reached the place, we saw there was a temple, but did not know what god they worshipped. There was a wide open space in front of the temple where they had erected a provisional theatrical stage, with painted beams and square pillars, which looked very imposing at a distance, but at close range were found to consist of painted paper wrapped around the poles and varnished over with paint.

　　锣声忽至，四人抬对烛，大如断柱，八人抬一猪，大若牯牛，盖公养十二年始宰以献神。策廷笑曰："猪固寿长，神亦齿利；我若为神，乌能享此。"余曰："亦足见其愚诚也。"

　　入庙，殿廊轩院所设花果盆玩，并不剪枝拗节，尽以苍老古怪为佳，大半皆黄山松。既而开场演剧，人如潮涌而至，余与策廷遂避去。未两载，余与同事不合，拂衣归里。

　　余自绩溪之游，见热闹场中卑鄙之状不堪入目，因易儒为贾。余有姑丈袁万九，在盘溪之仙人塘作酿酒生涯。余与施心耕附资合伙。袁酒本海贩。不一载，值台湾林爽文之乱，海道阻隔，货积本折。不得已，仍为"冯妇"。馆江北四年，一无快游可记。

Suddenly gongs were struck and there were four men carrying a pair of candles as big as broken pillars, and eight persons carrying a pig about the size of a young calf. This pig, it was pointed out to me, had been raised and kept by the village in common for twelve years expressly for this occasion to be used as an offering to the god. Ch'eht'ing laughed and said. "This pig's life is long, isn't it? but the god's teeth must also be sharp enough to bite it, mustn't they? I don't think I could enjoy such a huge pig, if I were a god." "However, it shows the religious devotion of the villagers," said I.

We entered the temple and saw the court and corridors were filled up with potted flowers and trees. These had not been artificially trained, but were chosen for their rugged and strange lines in their natural state, being mostly pine-trees from the Yellow Mountains, I believe. Then the theatrical performances began and the place was crowded full with people and we went away to avoid the noise and commotion. In less than two years, however, I left the place owing to differences of opinion with some of my colleagues, and returned home.

During my stay at Chich'i, I saw how unspeakably dirty politics was and how low men could stoop in official life, which made me decide to change my profession from scholar to businessman. I had a paternal uncle by marriage by the name of Yüan Wanchiu, who was a wine brewer by profession, living at the Fairy Pond of P'anch'i. I then went into this business with Shih Hsinkeng as partner. Yüan's wines were sold chiefly overseas, and in less than one year there came the rebellion of Lin Shuangwen in Formosa, traffic on the sea was interrupted, and we lost money. I was then compelled to return to my profession as a salaried man, in which capacity I stayed four years in Kiangpei,[1] during which period I did not enjoy any travel worth recording.

[1] A collective name given to such districts in Kiangsu as lie to the north of the Yangtze River, —Yangchow, Icheng, Taichow, Taihing, Tsingkiang, Nantungchow, etc. being among these districts.

　　迨居萧爽楼，正作烟火神仙。有表妹倩徐秀峰自粤东归，见余闲居，慨然曰："足下待露而爨，笔耕而炊，终非久计。盍偕我作岭南游？当不仅获蝇头利也。"芸亦劝余曰："乘此老亲尚健，子尚壮年，与其商柴计米而寻欢，不如一劳而永逸。"

　　余乃商诸交游者，集资作本，芸亦自办绣货，及岭南所无之苏酒醉蟹等物，禀知堂上，于小春十日，偕秀峰由东坝出芜湖口。长江初历，大畅襟怀。每晚，舟泊后，必小酌船头。见捕鱼者罾幂不满三尺，孔大约有四寸，铁箍四角，似取易沉。

Afterwards we were staying at the Hsiaoshuanglou, living like fairies on earth. The husband of my girl cousin, Hsü Hsiufeng, then happened to return from Eastern Kwangtung. Seeing that I was out of a job, he said to me, "I don't see how you can get along forever living by your pen and making your breakfast out of morning dew. Why don't you come along with me to Lingnan [Central Kwangtung]? I am sure you can make a lot of money there." Yün also approved and said to me, "I think you should go while our parents are still strong and you are still in your prime. It is better to make some money once for all than to live from hand to mouth like this."

I then got together some capital with the help of my friends for this venture, and Yün also personally attended to the purchase of embroidered goods, Soochow wine and winetreated crabs, things that were not produced in Kwangtung. With the permission of my parents, I started on the tenth of the tenth moon with Hsiufeng, going by way of Tungpa and coming upon the Yangtze at Wuhu. This being my first trip up the Yangtze, it gave me quite a thrill. Every night when the boat lay at anchor, I would have a little drink on the bow of the boat. Once I saw a fisherman carrying a little net hardly three feet wide; the meshes were about four inches wide and its four corners were tied with strips of iron, which were apparently used as sinkers.

　　余笑曰:"圣人之教,虽曰'罟不用数,'而如此之大孔小罾,焉
能有获?"秀峰曰:"此专为网鳊鱼设也。"见其系以长绳,忽起忽落,
似探鱼之有无。未几,急挽出水,已有鳊鱼枷罾孔而起矣。余始喟然曰:
"可知一己之见,未可测其奥妙!"

　　一日,见江心中一峰突起,四无依倚。秀峰曰:"此小孤山也。"
霜林中,殿阁参差;乘风径过,惜未一游。至滕王阁,犹吾苏府学之
尊经阁移于胥门之大马头,王子安序中所云不足信也。

　　即于阁下换高尾昂首船,名"三板子,"由赣关至南安登陆。值
余三十诞辰,秀峰备面为寿。

"Although Mencius told us that a fishing net should not be too fine," I said, chuckling, "I don't see how they are going to catch any fish with such big meshes and a tiny net." Hsiufeng explained that this kind was made specially for catching *pien* fish. I noticed the net was tied to a long rope and let down into the water every now and then, as if trying to see if there was any fish around. After a while, the fisherman gave a sudden pull and there was a big *pien* fish right enough caught in it. "It is true that one is never too old to learn!" I remarked with a sigh.

One day I saw a solitary hilly island rising abruptly from the middle of the river, and learnt from Hsiufeng that this was the famous "Little Orphan." There were temples and towers hidden among the frost-covered wood, but unfortunately we were prevented from visiting the place, as our boat was passing by very fast with the wind. When arriving at the famous Tower of Prince T'eng, I realized that the geographical reference to this Tower contained in the sketch by Wang Tzǔ-an was entirely erroneous, just as the location of the Chunching Tower of Soochow was changed to the Main Wharf of the Hsümen Gate.

We then embarked at the Tower on a "sampan" with upturned bow and stern, and sailed up past Kungkuan as far as Nan-an, where we left the boat. The day of my arrival there happened to be my thirtieth birthday and Hsiufeng prepared a dinner of noodles in my honour.

　　越日过大庾岭，山巅一亭，匾曰"举头日近"，言其高也。山头分为二。两边峭壁，中留一道如石巷。口列两碑：一曰"急流勇退"，一曰"得意不可再往"。山顶有梅将军祠，未考为何朝人。所谓岭上梅花，并无一树，意者以梅将军得名梅岭耶？余所带送礼盆梅，至此将交腊月，已花落而叶黄矣。

　　过岭出口，山川风物便觉顿殊。岭西一山，石窍玲珑，已忘其名，舆夫曰："中有仙人床榻"。匆匆竟过，以未得游为怅。

Next day we passed the Tayü Pass[1]. On the top of the Pass there was a pavilion with a signboard reading: "The sun hangs quite near over our heads," referring to the height of the place. The peak here was split in twain by a perpendicular cleavage in the cliffs which rose up like walls, leaving a path in the centre like a stone alleyway. There were two stone inscriptions at the entrance to the Pass, one bearing the words, "Retreat heroically before a rushing torrent" and the other containing the wise counsel: "Be satisfied with your luck this time." There was a temple on top in honour of a certain General Mei, I do not know of what dynasty.[2] I do not know what people mean by speaking of "plum flowers on the Pass," because I did not see a single plum-tree there; perhaps it was called the "*Mei* (plum) Peak" after General Mei. The twelfth and last moon was there and the pots of plum flowers which I had brought along as gifts to friends had already blossomed and the flowers had fallen off and the leaves turned yellow.

Coming out on the other side of the Pass, I saw an entirely different type of scenery. On the west there was a hill with beautiful rocks, whose name I have forgotten, and I was informed by my sedan-chair bearers that there was a "Fairy's Bed" on it, which I had to forego the pleasure of visiting, as I was in a hurry to proceed on my way.

[1] This is the pass on the frontier between Kwangsi and Kwangtung. — *Tr.*
[2] This was General Mei Chüan who was one of the first Chinese colonizers of Kwangtung at the beginning of the Han Dynasty. — *Tr.*

　　至南雄，雇老龙船。过佛山镇，见人家墙顶多列盆花，叶如冬青，花如牡丹，有大红，粉白，粉红三种，盖山茶花也。

　　腊月望，始抵省城，寓靖海门内，赁王姓临街楼屋三椽。秀峰货物皆销与当道，余亦随其开单拜客。即有配礼者，络绎取货，不旬日而余物已尽。除夕蚊声如雷。岁朝贺节，有棉袍纱套者。不惟气候迥别，即土著人物同一五官，而神情迥异。

　　正月既望，有署中同乡三友拉余游河观妓，名曰"打水围"，妓名"老举"。于是同出靖海门，下小艇，如剖分之半蛋而加篷焉。

On reaching Nanhsiung, we engaged an old "dragon boat." At the Buddhist Hill Hamlet, I saw that over the top of the walls of people's homes were placed many potted flowers, whose leaves were like *Ilex pedunculosa* and whose flowers were like peony, in three different colours of red, pink and white. These were camelias.

We reached Canton on the fifteenth of the twelfth moon and stayed inside the Tsinghai Gate, where we rented a three-roomed flat on the street from one Mr. Wang. Hsiufeng's customers were all local officials, and I accompanied him on his rounds of official calls. There were then many people who came to buy our goods for weddings and other ceremonial occasions, and in less than ten days all my stocks were sold. On the New Year's Eve, there were still plenty of mosquitoes humming like thunder. People wore padded gowns with crape gowns on top during the New Year calls, and I noticed that not only was the climate here so different, but that even the native inhabitants, who had assuredly the same anatomy as ours, had such a different facial expression.

On the sixteenth of the first moon, I was asked by three friends of my native district working in the yamen to go and see the singsong girls on the river—a custom which was called "making rounds on the river." The prostitutes were called "laochü." Coming out by the Tsinghai Gate, we went down little boats which looked like egg-shells cut in two, covered with a roof-matting.

　　先至沙面，妓船名"花艇"，皆对头分排，中留水巷，以通小艇往来。
每帮约一二十号，横木绑定，以防海风。两船之间钉以木桩，套以籐
圈，以便随潮长落。鸨儿呼为"梳头婆"，头用银丝为架，高约四寸许，
空其中而蟠发于外，以长耳挖插一朵花于鬓，身披元青短袄，著元青
长裤，管拖脚背，腰束汗巾，或红或绿，赤足撒鞋，式如梨园旦脚；
登其艇，即躬身笑迎，寋怖入舱。旁列椅机，中设大炕，一门通躺后。
妇呼有客，即闻履声杂沓而出。有挽髻者，有盘辫者；傅粉如粉墙，
搽脂如榴火；或红袄绿裤，或绿袄红裤，有著短袜而撮绣花蝴蝶履者，
有赤足而套银脚镯者；或蹲于炕，或倚于门，双瞳闪闪，一言不发。

First we came to Shameen where the sing-song boats, called "flower boats," were anchored in two parallel rows with a clear space in the centre for small boats to pass up and down. There were ten or twenty boats in one group, which were all tied up to horizontal logs to secure them against high wind. Between the boats there were wooden piles sunk into the bottom of the river, with moveable rattan rings on top allowing the boats to rise and fall with tide. The woman keeper of these singsong girls was called "shut'oup'o," whose hair was done up in a high coiffure by being wound round a hollow rack of silver wires over four inches high. One of her temples was decorated with a flower held there by means of a long "ear pick," and she wore a black jacket and long black trousers coming down to the instep of the foot, set in contrast by sashes of green or red tied round her waist. She wore slippers without stockings like an actress on the stage, and when people came down to the boat, she would bow them in with a smile and lift the curtain for them to enter the cabin. There were chairs and stools on the sides and a big divan in the centre, with a door leading into the stern of the boat. As soon as the woman shouted "Welcome guests!" we heard a confusion of footsteps of girls coming out. Some had regular coiffures, and some had their queues done up on top of their heads, all powdered like white-washed walls and rouged like the fiery pomegranate flowers; some in red jackets and green trousers and others in green jackets and red trousers; some bare-footed and wearing silver bracelets on their ankles and others in short socks and embroidered "butterfly-shoes"; again some squatting on the divan and some leaning against the door, and all looking attentively but silently at us.

　　余顾秀峰曰:"此何为者也?"秀峰曰:"目成之后，招之始相就耳。"
余试招之，果即欢容至前，袖出槟榔为敬。入口大嚼，涩不可耐，急吐之，
以纸擦唇，其吐如血。合艇皆大笑。

　　又至军工厂，妆束亦相等，维长幼皆能琵琶而已，与之言，对曰:
"噎?""噎"者，"何"也。

　　余曰:"少不入广者，以其销魂耳，若此野妆蛮语，谁为动心哉!"

　　一友曰:"潮帮妆束如仙，可往一游。"

　　至其帮，排舟亦如沙面。有著名鸨儿素娘者，妆束如花鼓妇。其
粉头衣皆长领，颈套项锁，前发齐眉，后发垂肩，中挽一髻，似丫髻，
裹足者著裙，不裹足者短袜，亦著蝴蝶履，长拖裤管，语音可辨;而
余终嫌为异服，兴趣索然。

I turned to Hsiufeng and said, "What is all this for?" "They are for you to choose," said Hsiufeng. "Call any one of them that you like and she will come up to you." I then beckoned to one, and she came forward with a smiling face and offered me a betelnut. I took a bite and, finding it to be most harsh and unpalatable, spat it out. While attempting to clean my lips with a piece of paper I saw it was besmeared with red like blood, and this conduct of mine aroused a great laughter from the whole company.

We then passed on to the Arsenal, and found the girls at the latter place to be dressed in the same costume, except that all of them, old and young, could play the *p'ip'a*. When I spoke to them, they would answer "Mi-eh?" which means "What is it?"

"People say that one should not come to Kwangtung in one's youth, only for fear of being enticed by sing-song girls," I said. "But when I look at these with their uncouth dresses and their barbarian dialect, I don't see where's the danger."

"The Swatow girls," said a friend of mine, "are dressed exquisitely. You might have a look there."

When we went there, we found the boats to be tied up in rows as at Shameen. There was a well-known brothel keeper called Su-niang, who was dressed like a woman in a Chinese circus. The girls' dresses had high collars, with silver locks hanging round their necks; their hair came down as far as the eyebrows in front and reached the shoulders at the back, with a coiffure on top looking like a maid-servant's coils: those with bound feet wore petticoats and the others wore short socks and also "butterfly-shoes" beneath their long slim pants. Their dialect was barely intelligible to me, but I disliked the strange costume and was not interested.

　　秀峰曰："靖海门对渡有扬帮，皆吴妆。君往，必有合意者。"

　　一友曰："所谓扬帮者，仅一鸨儿，呼曰'邵寡妇'，携一媳曰'大姑'，系来自扬州；余皆湖，广，江西人也。"

　　因至扬帮，对面两排仅十余艇。其中人物皆云鬟雾鬓，脂粉薄施。阔袖长裙，语音了了。所谓邵寡妇者殷勤相接。遂有一友另唤酒船——大者曰"恒艒，"小者曰"沙姑艇"——作东道相邀，请余择妓。余择一雏年者，身材状貌有类余妇芸娘，而足极尖细，名喜儿。秀峰唤一妓，名翠姑。余皆各有旧交。放艇中流，开怀畅饮，至更许；余恐不能自持，坚欲回寓，而城已下钥久矣。盖海疆之城，日落即闭，余不知也。

"You know there are Yangchow sing-song girls across the river from the Tsinghai Gate," said Hsiufeng, "and they are all in Soochow dress. I am sure if you go, you will find someone to your liking."

"This so-called Yangchow group," explained a friend, "consists only of a brothel keeper called 'Widow Shao' and her daughter-in-law called Big Missie, who really come from Yangchow; the rest of the girls all came from Kiangsi, Hunan, Hupeh and Kwangtung."

We then went to see these Yangchow girls, and saw that there were only about a dozen boats tied up in two rows opposite each other. The girls here had all puffy coiffures, broad sleeves and long petticoats, were slightly powdered and rouged and spoke an intelligible dialect to me. This so-called "Widow Shao" was very cordial to us. One of my friends then called a "wine boat," of which the bigger kind were called "henglou" and the smaller kind "shakut'ing." He wanted to be the host and asked me to choose my girl. I chose a very young one, called Hsi-erh, who had a pair of very small feet and whose figure and expression resembled Yün's, while Hsiufeng called a girl by the name of Ts'uiku, and the rest of the company asked for their old acquaintances. We then let the boat anchor in the middle of the river and had a wine feast lasting until about nine o'clock. I was afraid that I might not be able to control myself and insisted on going home, but the city gate had been locked up at sundown, in accordance with the custom on the coast cities, of which I was informed for the first time.

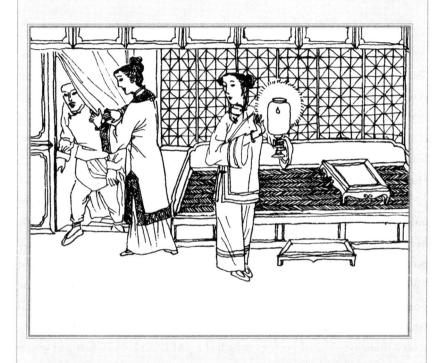

　　及终席，有卧吃鸦片烟者，有拥妓而调笑者。伻头各送衾枕至，行将连床开铺。余暗询喜儿："汝本艇可卧否？"对曰："有寮可居，未知有客否也。"（寮者，船顶之楼。）余曰："姑往探之。"招小艇渡至邵船。但见合帮灯火相对如长廊。寮适无客。鸨儿笑迎曰："我知今日贵客来，故留寮以相待也。"余笑曰："姥真荷叶下仙人哉！"遂有伻头移烛相引，由舱后梯而登，宛如斗室，旁一长榻，几案俱备。揭帘再进，即在头舱之顶，床亦旁设，中间方窗嵌以玻璃，不火而光满一室，盖对船之灯光也。衾帐镜奁，颇极华美。

At the end of the dinner, some were lying on the couch smoking opium, and some were fooling round with the girls. "Brothel attendants" began to bring in beddings and were going to make the beds for us to put up there for the night—all in the same cabin. I secretly asked Hsi-erh if she could put up there for the night. She suggested a "loft"—which was a cabin on the top of a boat— but did not know whether it was occupied. I proposed then that we might go and take a look, and got a sampan to row over to Widow Shao's boat, where I saw the boat lights shining in two parallel rows like a long corridor. The loft was unoccupied then and the woman welcomed me saying, "I knew that our honourable guest was coming tonight and have purposely reserved it for you." "You are indeed the 'Fairy under the Lotus Leaves'," I said, complimenting her with a smile. A "brothel attendant" then led the way with a candle in his hand up the ladder at the stern and came to the cabin, which was very small like a garret and was provided with a long couch and tables and chairs. Going through another curtained door, I entered what was the inner room, this being directly above the main cabin below. There was a bed at the side, and a square glass window in the centre admitted light from the neighbouring boats, so that the room was quite bright without a lamp of its own. The beddings, curtains and the dressing-table were all of a fine quality.

　　喜儿曰："从台可以望月。"即在梯门之上叠开一窗,蛇行而出,即后梢之顶也。三面皆设短栏。一轮明月,水阔天空,纵横如乱叶浮水者,酒船也;闪烁如繁星列天者,酒船之灯也;更有小艇梳织往来,笙歌弦索之声,杂以长潮之沸,令人情为之移。余曰:"'少不入广',当在斯矣!惜余妇芸娘不能偕游至此。"回顾喜儿,月下依稀相似,因挽之下台,息烛而卧。

　　天将晓,秀峰等已哄然至。余披衣起迎。皆责以昨晚之逃。余曰:"无他,恐公等掀衾揭帐耳。"遂同归寓。

"We can get a beautiful view of the moon from the terrace," Hsi-erh suggested to me. We then crawled out through a window over the hatchway and reached what was the top of the stern. The deck was bounded on three sides with low railings. A full moon was shining from a clear sky on the wide expanse of water, wine-boats were lying here and there like floating leaves, and their lights dotted the water surface like stars in the firmament. Through this picture, small sampans were threading their way and the music of string instruments and song was mixed with the distant rumble of the waves. I felt quite moved and thought to myself, "This is the reason why 'one shouldn't visit Kwangtung in one's youth!' Unfortunately my wife Yün is unable to accompany me here." I turned round and looked at Hsi-erh and saw that her face resembled Yün's under the hazy moonlight, and I escorted her back to the cabin, put out the light and we went to bed.

Next morning Hsiufeng and the other friends appeared at the cabin early at dawn. I hastily put on my gown and got up to meet them, but was scolded by everyone for deserting them last night. "I was afraid of you people teasing me at night and was only trying to get a little privacy," I explained. Then we went home together.

　　越数日，偕秀峰游海珠寺。寺在水中，围墙若城，四周离水五尺许，有洞，设大炮以防海寇。潮长潮落，随水浮沉，不觉炮门之或高或下，亦物理之不可测者。十三洋行在幽兰门之西，结构与洋画同。对渡名花地，花木甚繁，广州卖花处也。余自以为无花不识，至此仅识十之六七，询其名，有《群芳谱》所未载者，或土音之不同欤？

　　海幢寺规模极大。山门内植榕树，大可十余抱，阴浓如盖，秋冬不凋。柱槛窗阑皆以铁梨木为之。有菩提树，其叶似柿，浸水去皮，肉筋细如蝉翼纱，可裱小册写经。

A few days after this, I went with Hsiufeng to visit the Sea Pearl Temple. This was situated in the middle of the river and surrounded like a city by walls with gun-holds about five feet above the water in which were placed cannon for defense against pirates. As the tide rose and fell, the gun-holds seemed to shift up and down above the water level—an optical illusion which was truly amazing. The "Thirteen Foreign Firms" were situated on the west of the Yulanmen, or the Secluded Orchid Gate. The building structures looking just like those in a foreign painting. Across the water was a place called the "Garden Patch," being full of flower trees, for it was the flower market of Canton. I had always prided myself for knowing every variety of flower, but here I found that thirty or forty per cent of the flowers were unknown to me. I asked for their names and found that some of them were never recorded in the Ch'ünfangp'u ("Dictionary of Flowers"), perhaps accountable through the difference of dialects.

The Sea Screen Temple was built on a gigantic scale. Inside the temple gate, there was a banyan tree over ten fathoms in circumference, whose thick evergreen foliage looked like a green canopy. The railings and pillars of this temple were all made of "iron-pearwood." There was a linden tree whose leaves resembled those of the persimmon. One could scrape off the outer surface of these leaves after immersing them in water for some time, when the network of the fibre could be seen as fine as the wings of a cicada, and have them bound up into little volumes for the purpose of copying Buddhist texts.

　　归途访喜儿于花艇，适翠、喜二妓俱无客。茶罢欲行，挽留再三。余所属意在寮，而其媳大姑已有酒客在上。因谓邵鸨儿曰："若可同往寓中，则不妨一叙。"邵曰："可。"秀峰先归，嘱从者整理酒肴。余携翠、喜至寓。正谈笑间，适郡署王懋老不期而来，挽之同饮。酒将沾唇，忽闻楼下人声嘈杂，似有上楼之势。盖房东一仟素无赖，知余招妓，故引人图诈耳。秀峰怨曰："此皆三白一时高兴，不合我亦从之。"余曰："事已至此，应速思退兵之计，非斗口时也。"懋老曰："我当先下说之。"余急唤仆速雇两轿，先脱两妓，再图出城之策。

We looked for Hsi-erh among the "flower boats" on our way home, and it happened that both Ts'uiku and Hsi-erh were free. After having a cup of tea, we were going to leave but were begged again and again to stay. I had a mind to go to the loft again, but it was occupied at the time by a guest of Big Missie's, the widow's daughter-in-law. So I suggested to the widow that if the girls could come along to our house, I would be glad to spend an evening with them. The widow agreed, and Hsiufeng returned home first to order a dinner, while I followed later with the girls. While we were chatting and joking together, Mr. Wang Moulao of the local yamen unexpectedly turned up and was therefore asked to join us. We were just raising the wine-cups to our lips, when we heard a great noise of people downstairs, as if some men were attempting to come up. What really happened was that our landlord had a ne'er-do-well nephew who had learnt that we had brought sing-song girls to the house and was trying to blackmail us. Hsiufeng said regretfully, "This all comes of Sanpo's sudden desire for some fun.[1] I shouldn't have followed his example." "This is no time for argument," I said. "We must think of some ways and means to get out of the situation." Moulao offered to go down and speak to the people while I hastily instructed my servant to order two sedan-chairs for the girls to slip away first, and then see how we could manage to get out of the city.

[1] "Sanpo," the author's literary name, see p. 23, 1. 17 (Ch. I). — *Tr.*

　　闻懋老说之不退，亦不上楼。两轿已备，余仆手足颇捷，令其向前开路。秀挽翠姑继之，余挽喜儿于后，一哄而下。秀峰、翠姑得仆力，已出门去。喜儿为横手所拿。余急起腿，中其臂，手一松而喜儿脱去，余亦乘势脱身出。余仆犹守于门，以防追抢。

　　急问之曰："见喜儿否？"

　　仆曰："翠姑已乘轿去。喜娘但见其出，未见其乘轿也。"

　　余急燃炬，见空轿犹在路旁。急追至靖海门，见秀峰侍翠轿而立。又问之。对曰："或应投东，而反奔西矣。"急反身过寓十余家，闻暗处有唤余者，烛之，喜儿也；遂纳之轿，肩而行。秀峰亦奔至，曰："幽兰门有水窦可出，已托人贿之启钥。翠姑去矣，喜儿速往！"

We learnt that the people could not be persuaded to leave the house, nor were they coming up. Meanwhile, the two sedan-chairs were ready, and I ordered my servant, who was a strong, agile fellow, to lead the way; Hsiufeng followed him with Ts'uiku, while I and Hsi-erh brought up the rear thus we rushed downstairs, intending to break through. With the help of the servant, Hsiufeng and Ts'uiku disappeared outside the door, but Hsi-erh was caught by someone. I raised my leg and kicked the fellow's arm. Released from the hold, Hsi-erh dashed out and I escaped after her. My servant was standing guard at the door to prevent the rascals from pursuing us.

"Have you seen Hsi-erh?" I asked my servant.

"Ts'uiku has gone ahead in a sedan-chair," replied the servant, "and I have seen Hsi-erh come out also, but haven't seen her going into a sedan-chair."

I then lighted a torch and saw that the empty sedan-chair was still standing there. Hurriedly I rushed to the Tsinghai Gate and saw Hsiufeng standing there by the side of Ts'uiku's sedan-chair. In answer to my inquiry about Hsi-erh, he said that she might have gone off in an opposite direction by mistake. Quickly I turned back and passed a dozen houses to the west of our own before I heard somebody calling to me from a dark corner. I held up the light and saw it was indeed herself. I then put her in a sedan-chair and was starting, when Hsiufeng rushed to the place and informed me that there was a water-gate at the Yulanmen, and that he had asked somebody to bribe the gate-keeper.

余曰："君速回寓退兵。翠、喜交我。"

至水窦边，果已启钥。翠先在。余遂左披喜，右挽翠，折腰鹤步，跟跄出窦。天适微雨，路滑如油。至河干，沙面笙歌正盛。小艇有识翠姑者，招呼登舟。

始见喜儿首如飞蓬，钗环俱无有。

余曰："被抢去耶？"

喜儿笑曰："闻此皆赤金，阿母物也。妾于下楼时已除去，藏于囊中。若被抢去，累君赔偿耶？"

余闻言，心甚德之；令其重整钗环，勿告阿母，托言寓所人杂，故仍归舟耳。翠姑如言告母，并曰："酒菜已饱，备粥可也。"

"Ts'uiku has gone ahead, and Hsi-erh should follow immediately," he said.

"You leave the girls in my care, while you go home and try to talk the rascals down," I told Hsiufeng.

When we arrived at the water-gate, it had indeed been opened for us, and Ts'uiku had been waiting there. Holding Hsi-erh with my left arm and Ts'uiku with my right, I crawled out of the water-gate with them like fugitives. There was a light shower and the roads were slippery, and when we reached Shameen, the place was still full of music and song. Someone in a sampan knew Ts'uiku and called out to her to come aboard.

Only after going down the boat did I discover that Hsi-erh's hair was all dishevelled and all her hairpins and bangles had disappeared.

"Why, have you been robbed?" I asked.

"No," she smiled. "I was told that they are all solid gold and they belong to my adopted mother. I secretly put them away in my pocket as we were coming downstairs. It would be awful if I were robbed and you had to pay for the loss."

I heard what she said and felt very grateful to her. I then asked her to dress up again and not to tell her adopted mother about the whole incident, but merely to say that there were too many people in our house and that she preferred to come back to the boat. Ts'uiku told this to her mother accordingly, adding that they had had a full dinner and wanted only some congee.

　　时察上酒客已去。邵鸨儿命翠亦陪余登察。见两对绣鞋泥污已透。
三人共粥，聊以充饥。剪烛絮谈，始悉翠籍湖南，喜亦豫产，本姓欧阳，
父亡母醮，为恶叔所卖。翠姑告以迎新送旧之苦，心不欢必强笑，酒
不胜必强饮，身不快必强陪，喉不爽必强歌；更有乖张其性者，稍不
合意，即掷酒翻案，大声辱骂，假母不察，反言接待不周；又有恶客
彻夜踪蹰，不堪其扰。喜儿年轻初到，母犹惜之。不觉泪随言落。喜
儿亦默然涕泣。余乃挽喜入怀，抚慰之，嘱翠姑卧于外榻，盖因秀峰
交也。

By this time the guest at the loft had already left and the widow asked Ts'uiku also to accompany me to the room. I noticed that Ts'uiku's and Hsi-erh's embroidered shoes were already wet through and covered with mud. We three then sat down to have some congee together, in default of a proper evening meal. During the conversation under the candle-light, I learnt that T'suiku came from Hunan and Hsi-erh from Honan, and that Hsi-erh's real family name was Ouyang, but that after the death of her father and the remarriage of her mother, she had been sold by a wicked uncle of hers. Ts'uiku told me how hard the sing-song girls' life was: they had to smile when not happy, had to drink when they couldn't stand the wine, had to keep company when they weren't feeling well, and had to sing when their throats were tired; besides, there were people of a rough sort who would, at the slightest dissatisfaction, throw wine-pots, overturn tables and indulge in loud abuse and on top of that, the girls might receive all the blame, as far as the woman-keeper was concerned. There were also ill-bred customers who must continue their horse-play throughout the night until it was quite unbearable. She said that Hsi-erh was young and had just arrived, and the woman was very kind to her on that account. While recounting all her troubles, some tears had unconsciously rolled down Ts'uiku's cheeks, and Hsi-erh was also weeping silently. I then took Hsi-erh in my lap and comforted her, while I asked Ts'uiku to sleep in the outer room because she was a friend of Hsiufeng's.

　　自此或十日或五日，必遣人来招。喜或自放小艇，亲至河干迎接。
余每去，必邀秀峰，不邀他客，不另放艇。一夕之欢，番银四圆而已。
秀峰今翠明红，俗谓之"跳槽"，甚至一招两妓；余则惟喜儿一人。
偶独往，或小酌于平台，或清谈于寮内，不令唱歌，不强多饮，温存
体恤，一艇怡然。邻妓皆羡之。有空闲无客者，知余在寮，必来相访。
合帮之妓无一不识。每上其艇，呼余声不绝。余亦左顾右盼，应接不暇，
此虽挥霍万金所不能致者。

　　余四月在彼处共费百余金，得尝荔枝鲜果，亦生平快事。后鸨儿
欲索五百金，强余纳喜。余患其扰，遂图归计。秀峰迷恋于此，因劝
其购一妾，仍由原路返吴。

From this time on, they would send for us every five or ten days, and sometimes Hsi-erh would come personally in a sampan to the river bank to welcome me. Every time I went, I had Hsiufeng for company, without asking any other guests or hiring another boat, and this cost us only four dollars a night. Hsiufeng used to go from one girl to another, or "jump the trough," in the sing-song slang, and sometimes even had two girls at the same time, while I stuck only to Hsi-erh. Sometimes I went alone and either had a little drink on the deck or a quiet talk at the loft. I did not ask her to sing, or compel her to drink, being most considerate to her, and we felt very happy together. The other girls all envied her, and some of them, while unoccupied and learning that I was at the loft, would come and visit me. Thus I came to know every single one of them there, and when I went up the boat, I was greeted with a chorus of welcome. I had enough to do to give each a courteous reply, and this was a welcome that could not be bought with tens of thousands of dollars.

For four months I stayed there, spending altogether over a hundred dollars. I always regarded the experience of eating fresh *lichi* there as one of the greatest joys in my life. Later on, the woman wanted me to marry Hsi-erh for the sum of five hundred dollars. Her insistence rather annoyed me and I planned to return home. Hsiufeng, on the other hand, was very far gone with the girls, and I persuaded him to buy a concubine and returned to Soochow by the original route.

　　明年，秀峰再往，吾父不准偕游，遂就青浦杨明府之聘。及秀峰归，述及喜儿因余不往，几寻短见。噫！"半年一觉扬帮梦，赢得花船薄倖名"矣！

　　余自粤东归来，馆青浦两载，无快游可述。末几，芸憨相遇，物议沸腾。芸以愤激致病。余与程墨安设一书画铺于家门之侧，聊佐汤药之需。

　　中秋后二日，有吴云客偕毛忆香、王星澜邀余游西山小静室。余适腕底无闲，嘱其先往。

Hsiufeng went back there the following year, but my father forbade me to accompany him. After that, I accepted an invitation to work under Magistrate Yang of Tsingpu. On coming home, Hsiufeng recounted to me how Hsi-erh had several times attempted suicide because I didn't go back. Alas!

"Awaking from a half year's Yang-group dream,
I acquired a fickle name among the girls."[1]

During the two years at Tsingpu after my return from Kwangtung, I did not visit any place worthy of mention. It was soon after this that Yün and Han met each other and caused a great sensation among our relatives and friends, and Yün's health broke down on account of disappointment in Han. I had set up, with one Mr. Ch'eng Mo-an, a shop for selling books and paintings inside the gate of my own house, which helped somewhat to pay for the expenses of the doctor and medicine.

Two days after the Mid-Autumn Festival, I was invited by Wu Yünk'eh together with Mao Yi-hsiang and Wang Hsing-lan to go and visit the Little Quiet Lodge at the Western Hill. It happened then that I had an order to execute and asked them to go ahead first.

[1] This is an adaptation from two famous lines by Tu Mu. — *Tr.*

　　吴曰："子能出城，明午当在山前水踏桥之来鹤庵相候。"余诺之。
越日，留程守铺。余独步出阊门，至山前，过水踏桥，循田塍而西，
见一庵南向，门带清流。剥啄问之。应曰："客何来？"余告之。笑曰："此
得云也。客不见匾额乎？来鹤已过矣！"余曰："自桥至此，未见有庵。"
其人回指曰："客不见土墙中森森多竹者，即是也。"余乃返，至墙下，
小门深闭。门隙窥之，短篱曲径，绿竹猗猗，寂不闻人语声。叩之，
亦无应者。一人过，曰："墙穴有石，敲门具也。"余试连击，果有小
沙弥出应。

　　余即循径入，过小石桥，向西一折，始见山门，悬黑漆额，粉书"来
鹤"二字，后有长跋，不暇细观。

"If you will come along," said Wu, "we shall wait for you tomorrow noon at the Come Ye Storkes Temple by the Shuita Bridge at the foot of the hill." To this proposition I agreed, and on the following day, I asked Ch'eng to stay behind and keep shop for me, while I went on foot along. Passing through the Ch'angmen Gate, I reached the foot of the hill, went over the Shuita Bridge and followed the country path westwards until I saw a temple facing south, girdled by a clear stream outside its walls. Someone answered the door and asked me where I had come from. On being told the purpose of my visit, he informed me with an amused smile that this was the Tehyün Temple, as I might see from the characters on the signboard above the gate, and that I had already passed the Come Ye Storkes. I said that I had not seen any temple this side of the bridge, and then he pointed out to me a mud wall enclosing a bamboo thicket. I then retraced my steps to the foot of the wall, where I saw a small closed door. Peeping through a hole in the door, I saw some winding paths, a low fence and some delightfully green bamboo trees in the yard, but not a soul in the place. I knocked and there was no reply. Someone passed by and said to me, "There is a stone in a hole in the wall which is used for knocking." I followed his instruction and after repeated knocking, indeed an acolyte appeared.

I then went in along the path, passed a little stone bridge, and after turning west saw a monastery door with a black-varnished signboard bearing characters in white "Come Ye Storkes," with a long postscript which I did not stop to read.

　　入门经韦陀殿，上下光洁，纤尘不染，知为好静室。忽见左廊又一沙弥奉壶出。余大声呼问。即闻室内星澜笑曰："何如？我谓三白决不失信也。"旋见云客出迎，曰："候君早膳，何来之迟？"一僧继其后，向余稽首，问知为竹逸和尚。

　　入其室，仅小屋三椽，额曰"桂轩"。庭中双桂盛开。星澜、忆香群起嚷曰："来迟罚三杯！"席上荤素精洁，酒则黄白俱备。余问曰："公等游几处矣？"云客曰："昨来已晚，今晨仅到得云、河亭耳。"欢饮良久。饭毕，仍自得云、河亭共游八九处，至华山而止，各有佳处，不能尽述。

Entering it and passing through the Hall of Weit'ou the Swift-footed Buddha [defender of Buddhism against devils], I was struck by the extreme neatness and cleanliness of the place, and realized that its owner must be a person who loved quiet and solitude. Suddenly I saw another acolyte appear down the corridor on the left with a wine-pot in his hands. I shouted to him in a loud voice and demanded to know where my friends were. Then I heard Hsing-lan's voice chuckling in the room: "How about it now? I knew that Sanpo would keep his word!" Then Yünk'eh came out to welcome me and said, "We have been waiting for you to have breakfast with us. Why do you come so late?" Behind him stood a monk who nodded to me, and I learnt his monastic name was Chuyi.

I entered the room, which consisted merely of three beams, with a signboard reading "The Cassia Studio." Two cassia trees were standing in full bloom in the courtyard. Both Hsing-lan and Yi-hsiang got up and shouted to me, "You must be penalized three cups for coming late!" On the table, there were very nice, pretty vegetarian and non-vegetarian dishes, with both yellow and white wine. I inquired how many places they had visited, and Yünk'en told me that it was already late when they arrived the day before, and that they had visited only the two places Tehyün and Hot'ing that morning. We then had a very enjoyable drinking party for a long time, and after dinner we went again in the direction of Tehyün and Hot'ing and visited eight or nine places as far as the Huashan Hill, all beautiful in their own ways, but impossible to go into with full details here.

　　华山之顶有莲花峰，以时欲暮，期以后游。桂花之盛，至此为最。就花下饮清茗一瓯，即乘山舆，径回来鹤。桂轩之东，另有临洁小阁，已杯盘罗列。竹逸寡言静坐，而好客善饮。始则折桂催花，继则每人一令，二鼓始罢。

　　余曰："今夜月色甚佳，即此酣卧，未免有负清光。何处得高旷地，一玩月色，庶不虚此良夜也？"

　　竹逸曰："放鹤亭可登也。"

　　云客曰："星澜抱得琴来，未闻绝调，到彼一弹何如？"

　　乃偕往，但见木犀香里，一路霜林，月下长空，万籁俱寂。

There was a Lotus Peak on top of the Huashan Hill, but as it was already getting late, we promised ourselves we would visit it another time. At this spot, the cassia flowers reached the greatest profusion. We had a nice cup of tea under the flowers and then took moutain sedan-chairs back to the Come Ye Storkes Temple. A table was already laid in a little open hall, called Lin Chieh, on the east of the Cassia Studio. Monk Chuyi was by nature reticent, but a great drinker and very fond of company. At first we played a game with a twig of cassia,[1] and later each one was required to drink one round, and we did not break up till ten o'clock in the night.

"The moon is so beautiful to-night," I said. "It would be a pity to sleep in here. Can't we find a nice and high place, where we could enjoy the moon and spend the time in a way worthy of a night like this?"

"Let's go up to the Flying Stork Pavilion," suggested Chuyi.

"Hsing-lan has brought a *ch'in* along," said Yünk'eh, "but we haven't heard him play on it yet. How about going there and playing it for us?"

We then started together and saw on our way a stretch of trees enveloped in the silvery shadows of the night and buried in the fragrance of *Osmanthus fragrans*. All was peace and quiet under the moonlight and the universe seemed a stretch of long silence.

---

[1] This is a game similar to "Going to Jerusalem." A twig of cassia blossoms was passed round from hand to hand as long as the beat of the drum continued. The one found with the twig in his hand when the drum stopped beating was required to drink. — *Tr.*

　　星澜弹"梅花三弄"，飘飘欲仙。忆香亦兴发，袖出铁笛，呜呜而吹之。云客曰："今夜石湖看月者，谁能如吾辈之乐哉！"盖吾苏八月十八日石湖行春桥下，有看串月胜会，游船排挤，彻夜笙歌，名虽看月，实则挟妓哄饮而已。未几，月落霜寒，兴阑归卧。

　　明晨，云客谓众曰："此地有无隐庵，极幽僻，君等有到过者否？"咸对曰："无论未到，并未尝闻也。"

　　竹逸曰："无隐四面皆山，其地甚僻，僧不能久居。向年曾一至，已坍废。自尺木彭居士重修后，未尝往焉。今犹依稀识之。如欲往游，请为前导。"

Hsing-lan played for us the "Three Stanzas of Plum-Blossoms" with ethereal lightness. Caught by the gaiety of the moment, Yi-hsiang also took out his iron flute and played a low, plaintive melody. "I am sure," remarked Yünk'eh, "of all the people who are enjoying the moon tonight at the Shih-hu Lake, none can be quite as happy as we." This was true enough because it was the custom at Soochow for people to gather together under the Pacing Spring Bridge at the Shih-hu Lake on the night of the eighteenth of the eighth moon and look at the silvery chains of the moon's image in the water; the place was packed full with people in pleasure boats, and music and song were kept up throughout the night, but although they were supposed to be enjoying the moon, actually they were only having a night of carousal in the company of prostitutes. Soon the moon went down and the night was cold, and we retired to sleep after having thoroughly enjoyed ourselves.

The next morning, Yünk'eh said to all of us, "There is a Temple of Candour round about here in a very secluded spot. Have any of you been there?" We all replied that we had not even heard of the name, not to speak of having been to the place.

"This Temple of Candour is surrounded by hills on all sides," explained Chuyi, "and it is so entirely out-of-the-way that even monks cannot stay there for a long time. The last time I was there several years ago, the place was in ruins. I hear it has been rebuilt by the scholar P'eng Ch'ihmu, but have not seen it since. I suppose I could still locate the place. and if you all agree. I'll be your guide."

　　忆香曰："枵腹去耶？"

　　竹逸笑曰："已备素面矣。再令道人携酒盒相从也。"

　　面毕，步行而往。过高义园，云客欲往白云精舍。入门就坐，一僧徐步出，向云客拱手，曰："违教两月。城中有何新闻？抚军在辕否？"

　　忆香忽起，曰："秃！"拂袖径出。余与星澜忍笑随之。云客竹逸酬答数语，亦辞出。

　　高义园即范文正公墓。白云精舍在其旁。一轩面壁，上悬藤萝，下凿一潭，广丈许，一泓清碧，有金鳞游泳其中，名曰"钵盂泉"。竹炉茶灶，位置极幽。

"Are we going there on an empty stomach?" asked Yi-hsiang.

"I have already prepared some vegetarian noodle," said Chuyi laughingly, "and we can ask the 'waiting-monk' to follow us with a case of wine."

After eating the noodle, we started off on foot. As we passed the Garden of High Virtue, Yünk'eh wanted to go into the White Cloud Villa. We entered the place and had seated ourselves, when a monk came out gracefully and curtsied to Yünk'eh saying, "Haven't seen you for two months! And what's the news from the city? And is the Governor still in his yamen?"

"The baldhead snob!" said Yi-hsiang, and got up abruptly and swept out of the room. Hsing-lan and I followed him out, barely able to conceal our laughter. Yünk'eh and Chuyi remained behind to exchange a few words with the monk out of mere politeness and then also took leave.

This so-called Garden of High Virtue was the compound of Fan Chung-an's Tomb[1] and the White Cloud Villa was situated by its side. There was an open hall facing a cliff grown all over with ivy, with a pond of clear water over ten feet across below, which had goldfish in it and called "The Monk's Bowl Spring." With a bamboo-covered stove and a little fire-place for boiling tea, the place looked very nice and secluded indeed.

[1] Fan Chung-an, an upright prime minister of the Sung Dynasty. — *Tr.*

　　轩后于万绿丛中，可瞰范园之概，惜衲子俗，不堪久坐耳。

　　是时，由上沙村过鸡笼山，即余与鸿干登高处也。风物依然，鸿干已死，不胜今昔之感！正惆怅间，忽流泉阻路，不得进。有三五村童掘菌子于乱草中，探头而笑，似讶多人之至此者。询以无隐路。对曰："前途水大不可行。请返数武，南有小径，度岭可达。"从其言。度岭南行里许，渐觉竹树丛杂，四山环绕，径满绿茵，已无人迹。竹逸徘徊四顾，曰："似在斯而径不可辨，奈何？"余乃蹲身细瞩，于千竿竹中隐隐见乱石墙舍，径拨丛竹间，横穿入觅之，始得一门，曰："无隐禅院，某年月日南园老人彭某重修。"众喜，曰："非君则武陵源矣！"

From amongst the wild growth of green trees behind the hall, one could get a general view of Fan's Tomb, but, unfortunately, we could not suffer the vulgarity of the monk and had to leave sooner than we wanted.

We then went on to the Chicken Coop Hill through the Shangsha Village, which, it will be remembered, was the place I had visited in the company of Hungkan on a certain Double Ninth Festival Day. The same scenery was still there, as serene as ever, but Hungkan was dead, and I felt quite touched by the changes of human life. While occupied in this sad meditation, I suddenly saw there was a stream of water blocking our way. Four or five country lads were picking mushrooms and peeping and smiling at us from behind the bushes, apparently surprised to find so many people in a place like this. On being asked the way to the Temple of Candour, they replied that the road was impassable on account of the flood, and that we had to retrace our steps, follow a small path to the south and climb over a pass on the hill-top. The advice was taken and after crossing the hill-top and going on for over a *li*, we found ourselves lost in a thick wood of trees and bamboos, with hills all round us in the distance and green moss on the path at our feet, and not a trace of a single human being to be seen. Chuyi looked all round and said, "I know the Temple must be somewhere round here, but I can't find the way to it. What should we do?" I then bent down and looked carefully and descried some rocks and temple walls and buildings behind the thick bamboo grove. Brushing past the undergrowth on our way we struck across and reached a gate, where a signboard read, "The Temple of Candour rebuilt by Mr. P'eng, 'Old Man of South Garden,' on such-and-such a date." They were all delighted and gave me full credit for finding the place.

　　山门紧闭，敲良久，无应者。忽旁开一门，呀然有声，一鹑衣少年出，面有菜色，足无完履，问曰："客何为者？"

　　竹逸稽首曰："慕此幽静，特来瞻仰。"

　　少年曰："如此穷山，僧散无人接待，请觅他游。"言已，闭门欲进。云客急止之，许以启门放游，必当酬谢。

　　少年笑曰："茶叶俱无，恐慢客耳，岂望酬耶！"

　　山门一启，即见佛面，金光与绿阴相映，庭阶石础苔积如绣。殿后台级如墙，石阑绕之。循台而西，有石形如馒头，高二丈许，细竹环其趾。

The Temple gate was closed and after knocking for a long time, no one came to answer the door. Then suddenly a side door was opened with a crash and a young man in tatters and a pair of broken shoes appeared, wearing a pale, anaemic complexion.

"What do you come here for?" asked the young man.

"We have heard that the place is so nice and secluded, and have come here to pay a visit," replied Chuyi courteously.

"In such a poor temple, the monks are all gone, and there is no one to entertain you. You had better go away and visit some other place." With this, the young man turned round and was going to shut the door. Yünk'eh quickly stopped him and promised to repay him for the trouble, if he would let us in.

"Pay me for what trouble? That is not the point," replied the young man laughingly. "I was only afraid of being rude, for we have not even got tea leaves here."

As soon as the Temple gate was opened, we saw the Buddha's face, whose golden colour mingled with the green shade of the trees, and on the steps and the stone structures there was a thick layer of moss like fine velvet. Immediately behind the Temple there were a series of steps going up almost perpendicularly like a wall and surrounded on top by stone balustrades. On the west of the terrace, there was a huge rock shaped like a monk's scalp over twenty feet high and surrounded below with fine bamboo trees.

　　再西折北，由斜廊蹑级而登。客堂三楹，紧对大石。石下凿一小月池，清泉一派，荇藻交横。堂东即正殿。殿左西向为僧房厨灶；殿后临峭壁，树杂荫浓，仰不见天。星澜力疲，就池边小憩。余从之。

　　将启盒小酌，忽闻忆香音在树杪，呼曰："三白速来！此间有妙境。"仰而视之，不见其人，因与星澜循声觅之。由东厢出一小门，折北，有石磴如梯，约数十级；于竹坞中瞥见一楼。又梯而上，八窗洞然，额曰飞云阁。四山抱列如城，缺西南一角，遥见一水浸天，风帆隐隐，即太湖也。倚窗俯视，风动竹梢，如翻麦浪。

Turning again west and then north, there was a winding corridor of up-going steps, on top of which there was a three-roomed house, which was the parlour, standing close opposite the huge rock. Beneath the rock there was a small crescent-shaped pond with beautifully clear water in it and filled with water-cress. On the east of the parlour was the temple proper, and on the left of the temple, facing west, were the monk's living quarters and a kitchen. At the back of the temple that was a steep cliff and the trees here grew so thick and cast such a heavy shade over the place that the sky was completely hidden. Hsing-lan, all tired out, began to lie down by the side of the pond for a little rest, which example I immediately followed.

We were going to open the case for a little drink when we heard Yi-hsiang's voice coming from the top of the trees shouting to us, "Sanpo, come quick! It is wonderful up here!" We looked up, but could not see him, and so got up to look for him in the direction of his voice. We passed through a little door in the eastern room, went north and then up a score of stone steps steep like a ladder, after which we saw a building in the midst of a bamboo thicket. Going upstairs, we found that the place was provided with windows on all sides and a signboard bore the words "The Tower of Flying Clouds." On all sides we were surrounded by a girdle of mountains like a city wall, broken only at the south-western corner where we got a glimpse of water joining the sky at the horizon with some sailing boats dimly discernible on it, this being the Taihu Lake. As we leaned over the window and looked downwards, we saw the bamboo trees bent before the wind in swaying billows like a wheat field bowing before a summer breeze.

　　忆香曰："何如？"余曰："此妙境也。"忽又闻云客于楼西呼曰："忆香速来！此地更有妙境。"因又下楼，折而西，十余级，忽豁然开朗，平坦如台。度其地，已在殿后峭壁之上，残砖缺础尚存，盖亦昔日之殿基也。周望环山，较阁更畅。忆香对太湖长啸一声，则群山齐应。乃席地开樽，忽觉枵腹。少年欲烹焦饭代茶，随令改茶为粥。

　　邀与同啖。询其何以冷落至此，曰："四无居邻，夜多暴客。积粮时来强窃，即植蔬果，亦半为樵子所有。此为崇宁寺下院，长厨中月送饭乾一石，盐菜一坛而已。某为彭姓裔，暂居看守，行将归去，不久当无人迹矣。"云客谢以番银一圆。返至来鹤，买舟而归。余绘《无隐图》一幅，以赠竹逸，志快游也。

"What do you think of it?" said Yi-hsiang. "Very fine, indeed," said I. Then we suddenly heard Yünk'eh shouting to us from the west of the tower, "Yi-hsiang, come quick! It is still more wonderful up here!" Accordingly we went downstairs again, turned west and after ascending another dozen steps, reached an open space like a flat terrace. This must have been the top of the cliff behind the temple, and there were piles of broken bricks and stone pedestals which indicated that a temple must have stood at this place before. Here one gained a still better view of the surrounding hills than at the tower. Yi-hsiang gave a long, loud halloo in the direction of the Taihu Lake, which was echoed by all the hills. We then sat on the ground and were going to have a drink, when we all felt we should have some food. The young man was going to boil some dried rice for us in place of tea, and we instructed him to cook congee instead.

We asked the young man to join us at the meal and asked him how it was that the place was in such a pitiful condition. "The temple stands completely alone here without neighbouring houses and there are many burglars at night," replied the young man. "Whatever food we have has often been stolen, and even the vegetables and fruit we try to grow here have half gone to enrich the wood-cutters. The place is a branch of the Ts'ungning Temple, and as such receives a monthly allowance of ten bushel of dry cooked rice and a jar of salted vegetables only. I am only looking after the place for the descendants of Mr. P'eng, the rebuilder of the temple, and shall be leaving very soon, when the place will be completely deserted." Yünk'eh gave him a Mexican dollar, and we returned first to the Come Ye Storkes and then came home by boat. I painted a picture of the Temple of Candour and presented it to Chuyi as a souvenir of the enjoyable trip.

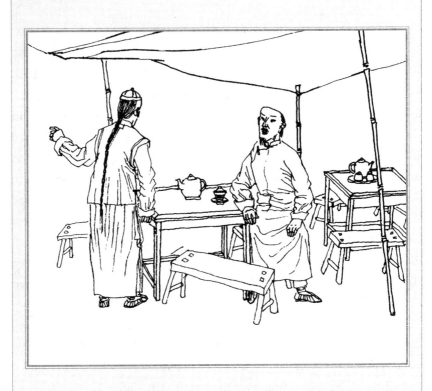

　　是年冬，余为友人作中保所累，家庭失欢，寄居锡山华氏。明年春，将之维扬，而短于资。有故人韩春泉在上洋幕府，因往访焉。衣敝履穿，不堪入署，投札约晤于郡庙园亭中。及出见，知余愁苦，慨助十金。园为洋商捐施而成，极为阔大，惜点缀各景，杂乱无章，后叠山石，亦无起伏照应。

　　归途忽思虞山之胜，适有便舟附之。时当春仲，桃李争妍，逆旅行踪，苦无伴侣。乃怀青铜三百，信步至虞山书院。墙外仰瞩，见丛树交花，娇红稚绿，傍水依山，极饶幽趣。惜不得其门而入。问途以往。遇设篷瀹茗者，就之。烹碧罗春，饮之极佳。询虞山何处最胜，一游者曰："从此出西关，近剑门，亦虞山最佳处也。君欲往，请为前导。"余欣然从之。

In the winter of that year, I incurred the displeasure of my parents on account of being the guarantor for a friend's loan, and moved to stay at Mr. Hua's home at Hsishan. In the spring of the following year, I wanted to take a trip to Yangchow, but was short of cash. There was an old friend of mine by the name of Han Ch'unch'üan who was working at the Shanghai yamen, and I therefore went to call on him. In the state of disreputable appearance that I was, I dared not call on him at the yamen, but sent a note asking him to meet me at a temple park. He turned up, and seeing the condition I was in, gave me ten dollars. This park was made with the money donated by an importer of foreign goods and occupied a very wide area; unfortunately its different structures lay about in a straggling manner, nor did the grottoes at the park have any compositional design.

On my way back, I suddenly thought of the beauties of the Yüshan Hill and took a boat which happened to be going there. This was in the second month of spring and the peach and pear trees were then in full bloom. My only regret was that I had no company on the road. I walked on foot to the Yüshan College with three hundred cash in my pocket. Looking in from the outside, I saw there was a profusion of trees and flowers in charming red and green, made all the more beautiful by a stream in front and a hill at the back. Unfortunately, I couldn't get in and asked someone for directions. Seeing a teashed there, I approached it and enjoyed a most wonderful cup of *p'iloch'un*. I made inquiries as to the places most worth visiting at the Yüshan Hill, and a visitor told me about a place near the Sword Gate outside the Western Pass, even offering to act as my guide, of which kindness I gladly availed myself.

　　出西门，循山脚，高低约数里，渐见山峰屹立，石作横纹。至则一山中分，两壁凹凸，高数十仞。近而仰视，势将倾堕。其人曰："相传上有洞府，多仙景，惜无径可登。"余兴发，挽袖卷衣，猿攀而上，直造其巅。所谓洞府者，深仅丈许，上有石罅，洞然见天。俯首下视，腿软欲堕。乃以腹面壁，依藤附蔓而下。其人叹曰："壮哉！游兴之豪，未见有如君者。"余口渴思饮，邀其人就野店沽饮三杯。阳乌将落，未得遍游。拾赭石十余块，怀之归寓。负笈搭夜航至苏，仍返锡山。此余愁苦中之快游也。

Following him past the Western Gate, I went along the foot of the hill for about several of undulating country, when a mountain peak with rocks in horizontal formations gradually came in view. On reaching the place, I saw perpendicular cliffs rising over a hundred feet high, with a sharp crack in the center, dividing, as it were, the mountain in two. When one stood under the cliff and looked upwards, it seemed as if it was going to fall down over one's head. My guide told me that, according to tradition, there was a fairies' cave on top with different wonderful views inside, but there was no road for going up. Unable to resist the temptation, I tucked up my sleeves and gowns and climbed up to the very top like a monkey. The so-called fairies' cave was only about ten feet deep, with a crack in its roof admitting a view of the sky. Looking down, however, my knees trembled and I felt as if I was going to fall down. I had, therefore, to come down with my belly against the cliff and gradually descended with the help of the creepers. This rather impressed my guide and beguiled him into exclaiming: "Bravo! I have never seen a fellow so adventurous as you!" The natural consequence was that, what with my thirst, I asked him to accompany me to a road shop for a sip. The sun was already going down and I had to turn back, carrying in my pocket a dozen brown pebbles that I had picked up at the place. That night, I took a boat back to Soochow and came home to Hsishan. This was a fascinating trip that I enjoyed in the midst of sorrow and adversity.

　　嘉庆甲子春，痛遭先君之变，行将弃家远遁，友人夏揖山挽留其家。秋八月，邀余同往东海永泰沙勘收花息。沙隶崇明。出刘河口，航海百余里。新涨初辟，尚无街市，茫茫芦荻，绝少人烟。仅有同业丁氏仓房数十椽，四面掘沟河，筑堤栽柳绕于外。

　　丁字实初，家于崇，为一沙之首户，司会计者姓王；俱豪爽好客，不拘礼节。与余乍见，即同故交。宰猪为馂，倾瓮为饮。令则拇战，不知诗文；歌则号呶，不讲音律。

In the spring of 1804 during the reign of Chiach'ing, I was about to leave home and become a recluse consequent upon the death of my father, when my friend Hsia Yishan kindly invited me to stay at his home. In the eighth moon of that year he asked me to accompany him to Tunghai, where he was going to collect crops from his farms at the Yungt'ai Beach. This sandy beach belonged to Ts'ungming *hsien* and was reached by the sea over a hundred *li* from Liuho. The beach had newly arisen from the bottom of the Yangtze River and been only recently cultivated; there were no streets yet and very little human habitation, and the place was covered with reeds for miles round. There was, besides Mr. Hsia, only one Mr. Ting who owned property there and had a grainage with over a score of rooms, which was surrounded on all sides by a moat and outside this, by an embankment grown over with willows.

Ting's literary name was Shihch'u; he came from Ts'ungming and was the head of the whole beach settlement. He had a shroff by the family name of Wang and these two were frank, jolly souls, being very fond of company, and treated us like old friends soon after our arrival. He used to kill a pig and provide a whole jar of wine to entertain us at dinner; at such drinking parties, he always played the finger-guessing game, being ignorant of any games of poetry, and, being equally innocent of any musical knowledge, used to crow when he felt like singing.

　　酒酣，挥工人舞拳相扑为戏。蓄牯牛百余头，皆露宿堤上。养鹅
为号，以防海贼。日则驱鹰犬猎于芦丛沙渚间，所获多飞禽。余亦从
之驰逐，倦则卧。

　　引至园田成熟处，每一字号圈筑高堤，以防潮汛。堤中通有水窦，
用闸启闭。旱则长潮时启闸灌之，潦则落潮时开闸泄之。佃人皆散处
如列星，一呼俱集，称业户曰"产主"，唯唯听命，朴诚可爱；而激
之非义，则野横过于狼虎，幸一言公平，率然拜服。风雨晦明，恍同
太古。

After treating himself to a generous drink, he would call the farm-hands together and make them hold wrestling or boxing matches for a pastime. He kept over a hundred head of cattle which stayed unsheltered on the embankments at night, and also a pack of geese for the purpose of raising an alarm against pirates. In the day-time, he would go hunting with his hawk and his hounds among the reeds and marshes, and return with a good bag of game. I used to accompany him in these hunts and lie down anywhere to sleep when tired.

Once he took me to the farms where the grains were ripe; these were all serially numbered and around each farm was built a high embankment for protection against the tides. This was provided with a lock for regulating the water level, being opened during high tide to let in the water when the field was too dry, and at low tide to let the water out when it was overflooded. The farm-hands' cottages were scattered all over the place, but the men could gather together at instant notice. These men addressed their employer as "master of the property," and were very obedient and charmingly simple and honest. Roused by any act of injustice, they could be fiercer than wild beasts, but if you said a word that appealed to their fair play, they could be just as quickly pacified. It was a life of simple struggle with the elements of nature, dreary and powerful and wild, like that of primeval times.

　　卧床外瞩，即睹洪涛，枕畔潮声如鸣金鼓。一夜，忽见数十里外有红灯，大如栲栳，浮于海中，又见红光烛天，势同失火。实初曰："此处起现神灯神火，不久又将涨出沙田矣。"揖山兴致素豪，至此益放。余更肆无忌惮，牛背狂歌，沙头醉舞，随其兴之所至，真生平无拘之快游也！事竣，十月始归。

　　吾苏虎邱之胜，余取后山之千顷云一处，次则剑池而已。余皆半藉人工，且为脂粉所污，已失山林本相。即新起之白公祠、塔影桥，不过留名雅耳。其冶坊滨，余戏改为"野芳滨"，更不过脂乡粉队，徒形其妖冶而已。

There one could see the sea from one's bed, and listen to the roaring waves that sounded like war-drums from one's pillow. One night I suddenly saw miles and miles away a red light, about the size of a big basket, bobbing up and down upon the high sea, and the horizon reddened as if illuminated by a great fire. "That is a 'spirit fire,'" said Shihch'u to me. "Its appearance is an omen that very soon more lands will rise up from the bottom of the river." Yishan was usually of a romantic turn of mind, and he became all the more abandoned and care-free in his ways here. In the absence of all conventional restraints, I would yell and sing on the back of a buffalo or, inspired by alcohol, dance and cavort on the beach and do anything my fancy dictated. This was the pleasantest and most romantic bit of travel that I ever enjoyed in my life. Business done, we left the place and came home in the tenth moon.

Of all the scenic beauties at Huch'iu of Soochow I like best "A Thousand Acres of Clouds," and next the Sword Pond. With the exception of these two places, they are all too much belaboured by human effort and contaminated by the atmosphere of social luxury, thereby losing all the quiet native charm of nature. Even the newly erected Pagoda's Shadow Bridge and the Temple of Po Chüyi are only interesting as preserving a historical interest. The Yehfangpin, which I playfully wrote with another three characters meaning the "Waterside of Rural Fragrance" is very much like sing-song girls who flirt with passers-by in their promenades.

　　其在城中最著名之狮子林，虽曰云林手笔，且石质玲珑，中多古木，然以大势观之，竟同乱堆煤渣，积以苔藓，穿以蚁穴，全无山林气势。以余管窥所及，不知其妙。

　　灵岩山为吴王馆娃宫故址，上有西施洞，响屧廊，采香径诸胜，而其势散漫，旷无收束，不及天平支硎之别饶幽趣。

　　邓尉山一名元墓，西背太湖，东对锦峰，丹崖翠阁，望如图画。居人种梅为业，花开数十里，一望如积雪，故名"香雪海"。

Inside the city, there is the famous Shihtsulin ("Lion's Forest"), supposed to be in the style of the famous painter Ni Yünlin, which, despite its many old trees and elegant rocks, resembles on the whole more a refuse heap of coal ashes bedecked with moss and ant-holes, without any suggestion of the natural rhythm of sweeping hills and towering forests. For an uncultivated person like myself, I just fail to see where its beauty lies.

The Lingyen Hill[1] is associated with the famous beauty of old Hsishih, who lived here as the court favourite of the King of Wu. There are places of interest on top like Hsishih's Cave, the Corridor of Musical Shoes and the Canal for Picking Fragrance. However, it is a straggling type of landscape, in need of some tightening, and is therefore not to be compared with the T'ienp'ing and Chih-hsing Hills in charm and beauty.

The Tengwei Hill is also known as "Yüan Tomb"; it faces the Chinfeng Peak on the east and the Taihu Lake on the west, and with its red cliffs and green towers, the whole hill looks like a painting. The inhabitants here plant plums for their living, and when the flowers are in bloom, there is a stretch of white blossoms for miles and miles looking like snow, which is the reason why the place is called "The Sea of Fragrant Snow."

[1] This and the following hills are all within a short distance of Soochow. — *Tr.*

　　山之左有古柏四树，名之曰"清、奇、古、怪。"清者一株挺直，
茂如翠盖；奇者卧地三曲，形同"之"字；古者秃顶扁阔，半朽如掌；
怪者体似旋螺，枝干皆然；相传汉以前物也。乙丑孟春，揖山尊人莼芗
先生偕其弟介石率子侄四人往幔山家祠春祭，兼扫祖墓，招余同往。顺
道先至灵岩山，出虎山桥，由贾家河进香雪海观梅。幔山祠宇即藏于香
雪海中。时花正盛，咳吐俱香。余曾为介石画《幔山风木图》十二册。

There are four old cypress trees on the left of the hill which have been given the four respective names, "Pure," "Rare," "Antique" and "Quaint." "Pure" goes up by a long straight trunk, spreading out a foliage on top resembling a parasol; "Rare" couches on the ground and rolls itself into three zigzag bends resembling the character *chih* (之); "Antique" is bald-headed at the top and broad and stumpy, with its straggling limbs half dried-up and resembling a man's palm; and "Quaint's" trunk twists round spirally all the way up to its highest branches. According to tradition, these trees were grown here as early as before the Han Dynasty. In the first moon of 1805, Yishan's father Shunhsiang, his uncle Chiehshih and four of the younger generation went to P'ushan Hill for the spring sacrifice at their ancestral temple as well as to visit their ancestral tombs, and I was invited to accompany them. We first visited the Lingyen Hill on our way, came out by the Hushan Bridge and arrived at the Sea of Fragrant Snow by way of the Feichia River to look at the plum blossoms there. Their ancestral temple at the P'ushan Hill was buried in this "Sea of Fragrant Snow" and in the all-pervading glory of the plum-flowers, even our coughs and spittings seemed perfumed. I painted twelve pictures of the trees and sceneries of the P'ushan Hill and presented them to Chiehshih as a souvenir.

　　是年九月，余从石琢堂殿撰赴四川重庆府之任。溯长江而上，舟抵皖城。皖山之麓，有元季忠臣余公之墓。墓侧有堂三楹，名曰"大观亭"。面临南湖，背倚潜山。亭在山脊，眺远颇畅。旁有深廊，北窗洞开。时值霜叶初红，烂如桃李。

　　同游者为蒋寿朋、蔡子琴。南城外又有王氏园。其地长于东西，短于南北，盖北紧背城，南则临湖故也。既限于地，颇难位置，而观其结构，作重台叠馆之法。

In the ninth moon of the same year, I accompanied his honour Shih Chot'ang on the voyage to his office at Chungking in Szechuen. Following the Yangtze up, we came to the Huanshan Hill, where was Yü's Tomb, belonging to a loyal Chinese minister at the end of the Mongol Dynasty. By the side of his tomb, there was a hall called the Majestic View Pavilion, a three-roomed affair, facing the South Lake in front and looking out on the Ch'ienshan Hill at its back. The Pavilion was situated on a knoll and therefore commanded an open view of the distance. It was open on the north side, and by its side was a long covered corridor. The tree leaves were just turning red, resplendent like peach and pear blossoms.

At this time Chiang Shoupeng and Ts'ai Tzuch'in were travelling with me. Outside the South Gate there was Wang's Garden, which consisted of a long narrow strip of land running east and west, being limited on the south by the lake and on the north by the city wall, presenting a most difficult problem for the architect. The problem was ingeniously solved, however, by having serried terraces and storeyed towers.

  重台者，屋上作月台为庭院，叠石栽花于上，使游人不知脚下有屋；盖上叠石者则下实，上庭院者则下虚，故花木仍得地气而生也。叠馆者，楼上作轩，轩上再作平台，上下盘折，重叠四层，且有小池，水不漏泄，竟莫测其何虚何实。其立脚全用砖石为之，承重处仿照西洋立柱法。幸面对南湖，目无所阻，骋怀游览，胜于平园，真人工之奇绝者也。

  武昌黄鹤楼在黄鹄矶上，后拖黄鹄山，俗呼为蛇山。楼有三层，画栋飞檐，倚城屹峙，面临汉江，与汉阳晴川阁相对。

By "serried terraces" is meant building of courtyards on the roof gardens, provided with rockeries and flower trees in such a manner that visitors would hardly suspect a house underneath; the rockeries standing on what was solid ground below and the courtyards on tops of buildings, so that the flowers actually grew upon the soil. And by "storeyed towers" is meant crowning an upper storey with an open tower on top, and again crowning the latter with an open terrace, so that the whole consisted of four storeys going from one to another in an artfully irregular manner; there were also small pools actually holding water at different levels so that one could hardly tell whether one was standing on solid ground or on a top floor. The basic structures consisted entirely of bricks and stone, with the supports made in the western style. It was fortunately situated on the lake, so that one actually gained a better unobstructed view of the surrounding country than from an ordinary garden on a piece of flat ground. This garden seemed to me to show a marvellous human ingenuity.

The Tower of Yellow Stork at Wuchang is situated on the Yellow Swan Cliff, being connected with the Yellow Swan Hill at the back, popularly known as the Snake Hill. The three-storeyed Tower with its beautifully painted eaves and girders, stood on top of the city overlooking the Han River in a way that counterbalanced the Ch'ingch'üan Tower at Hanyang on the opposite shore.

　　余与琢堂冒雪登焉。仰视长空，琼花风舞，遥指银山玉树，恍如身在瑶台。江中往来小艇，纵横掀播，如浪卷残叶，名利之心至此一冷。壁间题咏甚多，不能记忆。但记楹对有云：

　　"何时黄鹤重来，且共倒金樽，浇洲渚千年芳草。但见白云飞去，更谁吹玉笛，落江城五月梅花？"

　　黄州赤壁在府城汉川门外，屹立江滨，截然如壁，石皆绛色，故名焉。《水经》谓之赤鼻山。东坡游此作二赋，指为吴魏交兵处，则非也。壁下已成陆地，上有二赋亭。

I went up the Tower one snowy day with Chot'ang; the beautiful snow-flakes dancing in the sky above and silver-clad hills and jade bedraggled trees below gave one the impression of a fairy world. Little boats passed up and down the river, tossed about by the waves like falling leaves in a storm. Looking at a view like this somehow made one feel the vanity of life and the futility of its struggles. There were a lot of poems written on the walls of the Tower, which I have all forgotten with the exception of a couplet running as follows:[1]

"When the yellow stork comes again,
let's together empty the golden goblet,
pouring wine-offering
over the thousand-year green meadow
on the isle.
"Just look at the white clouds sailing off,
and who will play the jade flute,
sending its melodies
down the fifth-moon plum-blossoms
in the city?"

The Brown Cliffs of Huangchow are outside the Han River Gate, rising perpendicularly like a wall from the bank of the river, and so called because of the colour of their rocks. In *Shuik'ing* this is referred to as the "Brown Nose Hill." Su Tungp'o wrote two *fu*-poems when he visited this place, but through an error, referred to it as the scene of the river battle between the Wu and Wei Kingdoms. The cliffs are no longer standing immediately by the water, for there is land underneath, and on top there is the "Pavilion of the Two *Fu*-poems."

---

[1] In a Chinese couplet, which one sees everywhere in halls and parlours and temples, every word in one member must have a word of the same class but reversed tone in the corresponding position in the other member. With the exception of "the's", this can be seen in the translation given herewith. — *Tr.*

　　是年仲冬抵荆州。琢堂得升潼关观察之信，留余住荆州。余以未得见蜀中山水为怅。时琢堂入川，而哲嗣敦夫、眷属，及蔡子琴、席芝堂俱留于荆州，居刘氏废园。余记其厅额曰“紫藤红树山房”。庭阶围以石栏，凿方池一亩。池中建一亭，有石桥通焉。亭后筑土垒石，杂树丛生。余多旷地，楼阁俱倾颓矣。客中无事，或吟或啸，或出游，或聚谈。岁暮虽资斧不继，而上下雍雍，典衣沽酒，且置锣鼓敲之。每夜必酌，每酌必令。窘则四两烧刀，亦必大施筋政。

That year in the eleventh moon we reached Kingchow. Chot'ang had then received the news of his promotion to *taotai* at Tungkuan, and I was asked to stay behind at Kingchow, thus forfeiting an opportunity to see the beautiful hills and waters of Szechuen, to my great regret. Chot'ang went there alone, leaving me with Ts'ai Tzǔch'in and Hsi Chiht'ang and his son Tunfu and family. We were staying at "Liu's Old Garden," whose hall signboard, I remember, read: "The Mountain Hut of Wistarias and Red Trees." There were courtyards with stone balustrades and a square pond occupying one *mow* of space. In the centre of the pond there was a pavilion which was connected with the bank by a stone bridge and surrounded by grottoes and trees at the back. The rest mainly consisted of flat ground, the towers and structures being all in ruins. As we had nothing to do all day, we spent the time in singing, whistling, chatting together or making excursions to the neighbourhood. Although we were none too well provided in our pockets towards the New Year's Eve, we had a jolly time together by pawning our clothing to buy drinks, and even bought a set of drums and gongs to celebrate the New Year. We had wine every night and every time we drank we played wine-games; when hard pressed to it, we could still celebrate with four ounces of cheap, strong alcohol.

　　遇同乡蔡姓者，蔡子琴与叙宗系，乃其族子也。倩其导游名胜，至府学前之曲江楼。昔张九龄为长史时，赋诗其上。朱子亦有诗，曰："相思欲回首，但上曲江楼。"城上又有雄楚楼，五代时高氏所建，规模雄峻，极目可数百里。绕城傍水尽植垂杨，小舟荡桨往来，颇有画意。荆州府署即关壮缪帅府，仪门内有青石断马槽，相传即赤兔马食槽也。访罗含宅于城西小湖上，不遇；又访宋玉故宅于城北。昔庾信遇侯景之乱，遁归江陵，居宋玉故宅，继改为酒家；今则不可复识矣。

There we met a certain Ts'ai who came from the same district and, on an exchange of conversation, was found to be of the same clan with Ts'ai Tzŭch'in, but of an older generation. This Ts'ai was asked to act as our guide and took us to the Tower of Winding River in front of the college. This was the Tower where Chang Chiuning used to write poems when he was magistrate here. Chu Hsi also wrote two lines:

There shall I go, up the towering Tower of Winding River,
When of something I wish to refresh my memory that does wither.

On top of the city, there was also the Hsiungch'u Tower, which was a massive structure, being erected by the Kao's at the time of the Five Dynasties, and commanded a view of over a hundred miles to the distance. All the land round the city by the waterside was covered with weeping willows, and the place looked rather picturesque with small boats passing up and down. The Kingchow yamen was in itself the old headquarters of General Kuan Yü, with a broken stone trough of lapis lazuli inside the gate, which, according to tradition, was the trough where the famous Red Steed of General Kuan had fed. I tried to look round for the home of Lo Han on the little lake west of the city, but could not find it; and also tried to look for the old house of the poet Sung Yü north of the city. In this house of Sung Yü, Yü Hsin had lived, after he had run away from the capital during the rebellion of Hou Ching. It was said to have been used later as a wine shop, but was now nowhere to be found.

　　是年大除，雪后极寒。献岁发春，无贺年之扰。日惟燃纸炮，放纸鸢，札纸灯以为乐。既而风传花信，雨濯春尘。琢堂诸姬携其少女幼子顺川流而下。敦夫乃重整行装，合帮而走。由樊城登陆，直赴潼关。

　　由河南阌乡县西出函谷关，有"紫气东来"四字，即老子乘青牛所过之地。两山夹道，仅容二马并行。约十里即潼关，左背峭壁，右临黄河。关在山河之间，扼喉而起，重楼叠垛，极其雄峻，而车马寂然，人烟亦稀。昌黎诗曰："日照潼关四扇开，"殆亦言其冷落耶？

On New Year's Eve it snowed very heavily, and the weather was rather severe. During the New Year festival we were free from the redtape of New Year calls because of the snowfall but spent the days firing fire-crackers, flying kites and making paper lanterns to amuse ourselves. Soon the warm wind of spring awakened all the flowers and the spring showers moistened the earth, and Chot'ang's concubines arrived from up-river with his little sons and daughters. Tunfu then began to pack up and we started on the voyage north together, going on land from Fanch'eng, and went straight to Tungkuan.

Passing from the west of Wenhsiang *hsien* of Honan, we came to the Hankuokuan Pass, which Laotzǔ passed through on the back of a black cow when he was retiring from the world. There was an inscription which bore the words, "The Purple Air Comes from the East." The Pass consisted of a narrow foot-path between two high mountains, barely allowing two horses to go side by side. About ten *li* from the Hankuokuan was the Tungkuan Pass, with a perpendicular cliff at the back on one side and the Yellow River on the other. A fortress was erected at this strategic spot with a series of most imposing towers and ramparts, but there were few inhabitants around the place and hardly any traffic. The line which Han Yü wrote, "The sun is shining upon Tungkuan with its doors all open" seems also to refer to the desolate appearance of the place.

　　城中观察之下，仅一别驾。道署紧靠北城，后有园圃，横长约三亩。东西凿两池，水从西南墙外而入，东流至两池间，支分三道：一向南，至大厨房，以供日用；一向东，入东池；一向北折西，由石螭口中喷入西池，绕至西北，设闸泄泻，由城脚转北，穿窦而出，直下黄河。日夜环流，殊清人耳。竹树阴浓，仰不见天。

　　西池中有亭，藕花绕左右。东有面南书室三间，庭有葡萄架，下设方石，可弈可饮。以外皆菊畦。西有面东轩屋三间，坐其中可听流水声。轩南有小门可通内室。轩北窗下另凿小池。池之北有小庙，祀花神。

There was only a local commander besides the *taotai* at the city. The *taotai's* yamen lay close by the northern city wall, with a back garden and vegetable field about three *mow* long from right to left. On the east and west there were two ponds, with water running in from the south-west corner outside; it flowed east to a point between the two ponds where it divided up into three directions: one going south to the main kitchen for cooking purposes, another going east into the east pond, and the other turning north and then west and emptying itself through the mouth of a stone gargoyle into the west pond. Continuing from there, the water turned northwest where there was a lock, and then flowed northwards through a hole under the city wall until it joined the Yellow River outside. The unceasing rippling of the water close around day and night is quite delightful to the ear, and the heavy foliage of bamboos and trees here completely hid the sky from view.

There was a pavilion in the centre of the west pond standing amidst a profusion of lotus flowers. On its east bank, there was a studio of three rooms facing south, standing in a courtyard with a trellis of grape-vines, and beneath the trellis was a square stone table where one could drink or play chess. The rest of the place consisted of fields planted with chrysanthemum flowers. West of the pond, there was an open hall of three rooms facing east, where one could sit and listen to the flowing water. A little side door on the south led into a private residence. The north window looked out immediately on a small pond and across this, further north, was a little temple in honour of the Goddess of Flowers.

　　园正中筑三层楼一座，紧靠北城，高与城齐，俯视城外，即黄河也。河之北，山如屏列，已属山西界，真洋洋大观也。

　　余居园南，屋如舟式，庭有土山，上有小亭，登之可览园中之概。绿阴四合，夏无暑气。琢堂为余颜其斋曰"不系之舟。"此余幕游以来第一好居室也。土山之间，艺菊数十种，惜未及含葩，而琢堂调山左廉访矣。

　　眷属移寓潼川书院，余亦随往院中居焉。琢堂先赴任。余与子琴、芝堂等无事辄出游。

The main building of the garden was a three-storeyed affair lying in the centre close by the northern city wall and of the same height as the latter, from which one could look out upon the Yellow River outside the city. Beyond the river, a range of mountains rose up like a screen—in a territory belonging already to the Shansi Province—a most majestic sight.

I stayed in the southern part of the garden in a boat-shaped house, where there was a little pavilion on top of a mound, from which one could obtain a general view of the whole garden. The house was protected by the green shade of trees on all sides so that one did not feel the heat in summer. Chot'ang kindly named the studio for me: "An Unanchored Boat." This was the best house I ever lived in during the period I served as a yamen secretary. There were scores of varieties of cultivated chrysanthemums around the mound, but unfortunately we had to leave there on account of Chot'ang's promotion to an inspectorship in Shantung before the season for chrysanthemums came.

It was then that his family moved to the T'ungch'uan College where I accompanied them, while Chot'ang went to his office first. Tzŭch'in, Chiht'ang and myself were left without anything to do then and we often went for an outing.

　　乘骑至华阴庙。过华封里，即尧时三祝处。庙内多秦槐汉柏，大皆三四抱，有槐中抱柏而生者，柏中抱槐而生者。殿廷古碑甚多。内有陈希夷书"福"、"寿"字。华山之脚有玉泉院，即希夷先生化形蜕骨处。有石洞如斗室，塑先生卧像于石床。其地水净沙明，草多绛色，泉流甚急，修竹绕之。洞外一方亭，额曰"无忧亭"。旁有古树三株，纹如裂炭，叶似槐而色深，不知其名，土人即呼曰"无忧树"。

　　太华之高不知几千仞，惜未能裹粮往登焉。归途见林柿正黄，就马上摘食之。土人呼止，弗听，嚼之，涩甚，急吐去。下骑觅泉漱口，始能言。土人大笑。盖柿须摘下，煮一沸始去其涩，余不知也。

One day we went on horseback to the Huayin Temple, passing through the Huafeng Village, the place where old Emperor Yao prayed three times for his people. There were at the Temple many locust trees dating back to the Ch'in Dynasty and cypress trees of the Han Dynasty, mostly three or four fathoms in circumference, some locust trees growing inside a cypress, and some cypresses growing inside a locust tree. There were any number of old stone inscriptions in the different courtyards, with two in particular consisting of the two characters for "Good Fortune" and "Longevity" respectively written by Ch'en Hsiyi. There was a Jade Fountain Court at the foot of the Huashan Mountains where Ch'en had departed from this earth as a Taoist fairy. His image, in a couching position, lay on a stone bed in a very small cave. At this place, the water was very clear and the sands nice and clean; most of the vegetation was of a deep red colour and there was a very rapid mountain stream flowing through a thick bamboo grove. A square pavilion stood outside the cave with the signboard:"Carefree Pavilion." By its side were three old trees, whose barks were cracked like broken coal and whose leaves resembled those of the locust tree, but were of a deeper colour. I did not know their name, but the natives aptly and conveniently called them "care-free trees."

I have no idea how many thousand feet high the Huashan Mountains are and regret very much not having been able to pack up some dry provisions and go exploring them for a few days. On my way back I saw some wild persimmons, which were of a ripe colour. I picked one from the tree while on horseback, and was going to eat it then and there. The native people tried to stop me, but I wouldn't listen to them. Only after taking a bite did I find it to have a very harsh flavour. So much so that I quickly spat it out and had to come down from horseback and rinse my mouth at a spring before I could speak, to the great merriment of my native advisers. For persimmons should be boiled in order to take away their harsh flavour, but I learnt this a little too late.

　　十月初，琢堂自山东专人来接眷属，遂出潼关，由河南入鲁。

　　山东济南府城内，西有大明湖。其中有历下亭，水香亭诸胜。夏月柳阴浓处，菡萏香来，载酒泛舟，极有幽趣。余冬日往视，但见衰柳寒烟，一水茫茫而已。趵突泉为济南七十二泉之冠。泉分三眼，从地底怒涌突起，势如腾沸。凡泉皆从上而下，此独从下而上，亦一奇也。池上有楼，供吕祖像，游者多于此品茶焉。明年二月，余就馆莱阳。至于卯秋，琢堂降官翰林，余亦入都。所谓登州海市，竟无从一见。

（完）

At the beginning of the tenth moon, Chot'ang sent a special messenger to bring his family to Shantung, and we left Tungkuan and came to Shantung by way of Honan.

The Taming Lake is in the western part of Tsinan City in Shantung, with places of interest like the Li-hsia and Shuihsiang Pavilions. It was most enjoyable to go boating around the lake with a few bottles of wine, and enjoy the fragrance of lotus flowers under the cool shade of willow trees in summer. I went there, however, on a winter day and saw only a stretch of cold water against some sparse willow trees and a frosty sky. The Paotu Spring ranks first among the seventy-two springs of Tsinan. The spring consists of three holes with water gushing forth from underneath and bubbling up like a boiling cauldron, in strange contrast to other springs whose water usually flows downwards. There is a storeyed building on the pond, with an altar to Lüchu inside, where the tourists used to stop and taste tea made from the spring water. In the second moon of the following year, I secured a position at Laiyang. When in the autumn of 1807, Chot'ang returned to the capital [Peking] and degraded as a *hanlin*, I accompanied him there. And I never saw the so-called "mirage of Tengchow" [on the Shantung coast].

[FINIS.]

Chapter Five

EXPERIENCE

(MISSING)

卷五·中山记历（原缺）

Chapter Six

THE WAY OF LIFE

(MISSING)

卷六·养生记道（原缺）

WADE-GILES TO PINYIN CONVERSION TABLE

"威妥玛—翟理斯式拼音"(Wade-Giles Spelling System)：英国人威妥玛 (Thomas Wade, 1818-1895) 以拉丁字母为汉字注音，创立了威氏拼音法；后经英国人翟理斯 (H. A. Giles, 1845-1935) 稍加修订，合称威妥玛—翟理斯式拼音。中国清末至1958年汉语拼音方案公布前，威氏拼音应用较广；受写作时代所限，林语堂作品中专有名词均使用威氏拼音音译。下表为威氏拼音与汉语拼音的对照转换表 ——编者注。

声母:

p → b	p' → p	m → m	f → f
t → d	t' → t	n → n	l → l
g → g	k' → k	h → h	
ch → j	ch' → q	hs → x	
ch → zh	ch' → ch	sh → sh	j → r
ts → z	ts' → c	s → s	

韵母:

i → i	u → u	ü → ü	
a → a	ia → ia	ua → ua	
o → o	o → uo		
ê → e	ieh → ie	üeh → üe	
ai → ai	uai → uai		
ei → ei	ui → ui (uei)		
ao → ao	iao → iao		
ou → ou	iu → iu (iou)		
an → an	ien → ian	uan → uan	üan → üan
ên → en	in → in	un → un (uen)	ün → ün
ang → ang	iang → iang	uang → uang	
êng → eng	ing → ing	uêng → ueng	
ung → ong	iung → iong		
eh → ê	êrh → er		

其他

chih → zhi	ch'ih → chi	shih → shi	jih → ri
tzǔ (tsǔ) → zi	tz'ǔ (ts'ǔ) → ci	sǔ, szǔ, ssǔ → si	

ENGLISH WORKS BY LIN YUTANG